Twayne's English Authors Series

Sylvia E. Bowman, *Editor*

INDIANA UNIVERSITY

Michael Arlen

TEAS 174

Michael Arlen

Michael Arlen

By HARRY KEYISHIAN
Fairleigh Dickinson University

TWAYNE PUBLISHERS
A DIVISION OF G. K. HALL & CO., BOSTON

Library of Congress Cataloging in Publication Data

Keyishian, Harry.
  Michael Arlen.

  (Twayne's English authors series; TEAS 174)
  Bibliography: pp. 133–45.
  Includes index.
  1. Arlen, Michael, 1895–1956. I. Title.
PR6001.R7Z68   823'.9'12   74-20819
ISBN 0–8057–1011–6

MANUFACTURED IN THE UNITED STATES OF AMERICA

For My Parents

Contents

About the Author

Harry Keyishian is Professor of English at the Madison, New Jersey campus of Fairleigh Dickinson University, where he teaches courses in Elizabethan drama. He received his B.A. from Queens College and his M.A. and Ph.D. from New York University. His reviews of contemporary fiction have appeared in *Book World*; his articles on Armenian-American authors in *Ararat*. He has also contributed articles on Elizabethan drama to *English Language Notes* and *Studies in English Literature*.

Preface

Michael Arlen was a popular British novelist of the 1920s and 1930s who captured the reading and playgoing public with his 1924 best seller *The Green Hat* in a manner that was perhaps unique in the history of popular literature. In his period of greatest popularity, he wrote well-crafted stories about fashionable men about town; loose, romantic ladies; and moody adulterers; and he made a great deal of money. When he became a charming celebrity on both sides of the Atlantic, he was known as much for his style of life as for his writing. The pathway to this agreeable eminence was complicated and enriched by the fact that Arlen had been born Dikran Kouyoumdjian of Armenian parents in Bulgaria. From this unlikely conjunction of origins and ends came a remarkable career and a significant body of writing.

The first chapter of this study concerns the beginnings of his career and his contributions to English magazines, signed with his Armenian name, between 1915 and 1919; and it traces the transition in subject matter from polemics to romance. The second chapter deals with two early works, *The London Venture* and *"Piracy"*—the former, as a revealing document of his search for a literary voice and role; the latter, as his first true novel. Chapter 3 reviews his prodigious output of short stories between 1920 and 1925, and the discussion is arranged to reveal both their literary qualities and their pattern of attitudes. An extended discussion in Chapter 4 of *The Green Hat* accounts, I hope, for both the novel's amazing success and its artistic limitations. In the fifth chapter the play version of *The Green Hat* is discussed, as well as the attendant publicity in England and the United States and the effect of the tremendous public interest on Arlen's life.

Chapter 6 describes Arlen's serious venture in new directions. The introspective, semi-autobiographical short story "Confessions of a Naturalized Englishman" shows Arlen in a debunking frame of mind in regard to his earlier fiction. Chapter 7 deals with his political novels of the 1930s, whose dominant theme is the search for the sources of evil in man and in society. While these novels generally were not successes, included among them is the one I judge to be Arlen's best, *Man's Mortality*. The final chapter describes his activities from 1940 until his death, in 1956, and evaluates his career.

I was drawn to Arlen by my general interest in the 1920s, and the hope that I may, in view of the similarities in our backgrounds, be able to contribute something unique to a study of his career—a discussion of his life and works by one for whom his being Armenian was his *least* exotic aspect.

I would like to extend personal appreciation to Leo Hamalian of the City University of New York, who first suggested Arlen to me; to Jack Antreassian, former editor of the magazine *Ararat*, in which some of this material first appeared; and to the late Gorham B. Munson, a colleague for a year at Fairleigh Dickinson University and a great source of information about the 1920s Especially helpful were generous and well-informed correspondences with Daphne Fielding, Diana Forbes-Robertson, William Saroyan, Vincent Sheean and Professor Arthur C. Turner of the University of California, Riverside. Mark Owings provided some valuable bibliographical aid. Sylvia Bowman's editorial comments brought my attention to much that was awkward in my early draft. Two research grants from Fairleigh Dickinson University covered the cost of typing and copying out-of-the-way material. I thank my wife Marjorie, a partner in the enterprise, on whose knowledge, judgment, and tact I frequently relied.

Finally, I would like to thank Michael Arlen for permission to quote from his father's work.

HARRY KEYISHIAN

Madison, New Jersey

Chronology

1892 Sarkis Kouyoumdjian, fleeing Turkish persecution, brings his family from Armenia to Bulgaria.

1895 Dikran Kouyoumdjian (Michael Arlen) is born November 16, the youngest of a family of four sons and one daughter.

1901 The Kouyoumdjians arrive in England on February 4 to reside in Southport.

1913 After schooling at Malvern College, and a brief stay in Switzerland, Dikran Kouyoumdjian spends a short time as a medical student at the University of Edinburgh; then goes to London to live on an allowance of two pounds a week; is befriended by several people in the literary world, including D. H. Lawrence.

1916 Begins writing for *Ararat: A Searchlight on Armenia* and for A. R. Orage's *The New Age*.

1920 Later *New Age* pieces collected as his first book, *The London Venture*; hereafter publishes as Michael Arlen.

1921 *The Romantic Lady* (short stories).

1922 *"Piracy"* (novel). Name changed legally to Michael Arlen.

1923 *These Charming People* (short stories).

1924 *The Green Hat* (novel). *Dear Father* (play), starring Herbert Marshall, produced in London.

1925 *The Green Hat* (play version) produced in London (starring Tallulah Bankhead) and New York (starring Katherine Cornell). Visits United States, amid much publicity; travels to Hollywood to do screenwriting. *These Charming People* (play, starring Cyril Maude—the New York version, somewhat altered, of *Dear Father*). *May Fair* (short stories).

1926 West Coast production of *The Green Hat*, starring Ruth Chatterton. *Why She Was Late for Dinner* (one-act play, produced in London).

1927   In ill health; has reunion with D. H. Lawrence in Florence. Lawrence, working on third revision of *Lady Chatterley's Lover*, uses Arlen as model for Michaelis, the Irish playwright. *The Zoo* (play, in collaboration with Winchell Smith). *Young Men in Love* (novel).

1928   Marries Countess Atalanta Mercati in Cannes, May 1. A son, Michael John, is born 1930; a daughter, Venetia, born 1933. The family resides near Cannes.

1929   *Babes in the Woods* (short stories).

1931   *Good Losers* (play), in collaboration with Walter Hackett (produced in London, starring Marion Lorne). *Men Dislike Women* (novel).

1933   *Man's Morality* (novel).

1934   *Hell! Said the Duchess* (novel).

1937   *The Crooked Coronet* (short stories).

1939   *The Flying Dutchman* (novel). Arlen returns to England. Writes weekly column for London magazine *The Tatler*, November, 1939–May, 1940.

1940   Accepts post as Public Relations Officer for the Western Midlands Region in November.

1941   After a "question" is raised in Parliament on January 30 concerning his suitability for the post, Arlen resigns; sails for North America to rejoin his family.

1944   In Hollywood, writes *The Heavenly Body* (screenplay), in collaboration with Walter Reisch.

1946   Arlen settles in New York.

1956   He dies in New York on June 23.

CHAPTER 1

Becoming Michael Arlen

I   *From the Danube to the Thames*

A few years before his death Michael Arlen summarized his career, cleverly but too modestly, for a *New Yorker* interviewer: "I was a flash in the pan in my twenties," he said. "I had a hell of a good time being flashy and there was, by the grace of God, a good deal of gold dust in the pan."[1] Although much of Arlen exists in the remark—the wit, the graceful self-deprecation, and, above all, the sense of style—much, too, is missing: his seriousness of intent and of accomplishment and the signs of the complex, sometimes bitter process by which the man born Dikran Kouyoumdjian, of Armenian parents, in Bulgaria, became the Michael Arlen who was the English romancer and novelist of manners, the author of the scandalous novel *The Green Hat*, and the symbol, to many, of the sophisticated 1920s. How the contrary elements of his makeup were held together, what inner conflicts they caused, and how they enriched Arlen's consciousness are matters fully as interesting as any of his books; for, of all the stories Michael Arlen told, one of the most meaningful and universal was his own—the story of the stranger who worked his way from the periphery of a glittering society towards its center. That story he told only fitfully throughout his career, but it is worth piecing together.[2]

When the Kouyoumdjian family left Armenia in 1892, after one of the outbreaks of Turkish hostility against Armenians which were to continue and intensify in the years that followed, it established a successful import business in Plovdiv in southern Bulgaria. Sarkis Kouyoumdjian had three sons, Takvor, Krikor, and Roupen, and a daughter, Ahavni. On November 16, 1895, the youngest child, Dikran, was born in Ruse (Ruschuk) on the Danube. Despite the family's economic success, Bulgaria

13

evidently wasn't quite far enough from Armenia, or stable enough
in its own right, because the family moved again, this time to
England. It arrived on February 4, 1901, and settled for some
years in a large Armenian colony in Southport. Sarkis Kouyoumdjian eventually shifted his business interests to Manchester,
where he was joined by his older sons, but branches of the
family enterprise existed as far away as South America.

Evidently Dikran was expected, like his brothers, to enter
the family business—he complains in an early essay about the
"Armenian" tendency to assume that a man not in trade was
somehow wasting his time—but, whatever his family's expectations, Dikran's interests lay elsewhere. He attended Malvern
College in Worcestershire, a school in those days said to be
more famous for cricketers than for scholarship or social advantage. He learned to speak with its accent, which an unsympa-
thetic acquaintance of his youth characterized as "the affected
drawl of the lesser public school,"[3] and he found life difficult
there because of his "exotic" background. When a schoolmate
snarled "Armenian Jew!" at him during dinner, Dikran—sure,
he said, that there was no such thing, but resenting the intended
insult—hit him on the head with a pot of jam. His punishment
for this violence was six cuts with a cane and the assignment
to write a Georgic. The faculty did poorly in coping with his
surname, which an Armenian would pronounce approximately
thus: "Dík-rahn Koo-yóum-john." "Now tell me, is it pronounced
Guimjun or Cowjan?" one of his masters used to joke. His master's
name, Arlen later recalled defensively, was Mugliston, but was
pronounced "Muggleston."[4]

Dikran was expected to attend Oxford; instead, as he put it
himself, "with a bowler hat crammed over my left ear and a
look of vicious obstinacy," he went to the University of Edinburgh, ostensibly to study medicine. "A silly mistake," he acknowledged, though he boasted that he gained from his education
"an utter inability to write poetry." He lasted at Edinburgh
only a short while because, as he has recalled this period, he
was "on the high road to general fecklessness," drank lots of beer,
couldn't settle down to a course of study, and deviated to
academic sidetracks like the study of Theosophy; but he pursued
that interest only to the point of handing out programs at an

Annie Besant lecture. He finally abandoned Edinburgh and, after a vacation in Switzerland, settled in London "'to take up a literary career,' my biographer will no doubt write of me," while living on an allowance of two pounds a week.[5]

When Dikran Kouyoumdjian arrived in 1913, London was a glittering city, a center of commerce, culture, and the Empire. But he was on the outside looking in, a stranger with an unpronounceable name and no career prospects:

> I am bitter about those first months, and will not easily forgive London for them; and if any young person shall begin to tell me how splendid were his first lonely days in the wilderness of people, how much he enjoyed the aimless wandering about the streets, . . . then I will turn on him and curse him for a fool or a knave. . . . An Armenian, who soon realises that his nationality is considered something of a *faux pas*, . . . comes to wonder why his fathers ever left Hayastan [Armenia]; for it seems to me much better to be a murdered prince in Hayastan than a living vagabond in London.[6]

With the outbreak of war in 1914 Dikran's problems were complicated by the fact that, as a Bulgarian by birth, he was ineligible for citizenship and military service.

After a time he made friends in the Bohemian quarters of London where writers, artists, exotics, and society folk could meet on somewhat even ground. He later recalled "teas at Golder's Green and Hampstead, and queerly serious discussions about sub-consciousness; 'rags' at Chelsea, and 'dalliance with grubbiness' and women." This social exchange was better than loneliness but, he discovered, not altogether pleasurable: "I do not like lying on the dirty floors of studios with candle grease dripping on me."[7] His literary friends were people of talent and fame, but somehow or other they were "beyond the pale," like D. H. Lawrence and Aldous Huxley, or they were striving to be, like the brilliant, rebellious Nancy Cunard, the daughter of the society hostess and music patron Lady Maud Cunard. Later Nancy Cunard became the main element in the character Iris March, the heroine of *The Green Hat*; but her actual life was far more adventurous than the fictional activities of Iris.

An Armenian coffeehouse on Shaftesbury Avenue was adopted by many of this group, especially when the larger restaurants

closed early in wartime. The Eiffel Tower Restaurant on Percy
Street, owned by a charming Viennese named Stulic, became a
favorite haunt of Nancy Cunard and her friends, who gathered
there to escape the observation of their parents. They called
their group the "Corrupt Coterie." In a poem about their "meet-
ings," ones presided over by Stulic himself, Nancy Cunard praised
the company as having "no lack / Of wits and glamour, strong
wine, new foods, fine looks, strange sounding language of divers
men."[8] Later Michael Arlen used the Eiffel Tower Restaurant
as the setting for several stories, but he renamed it the Mont
Agel. Perhaps Dikran Kouyoumdjian was entering society by
the back door; but through it he found the more interesting
people.

D. H. Lawrence was an important early influence and a
friend, though sometimes an impatient one. He found young
Dikran "blatant and pushing," he wrote; but he added, "that is
because he is *very foreign*, even though he doesn't know it
himself. In English life he is in a strange, alien medium and
he can't adjust himself. But I find the core of him *very good*.
One must be patient with his jarring manner, and listen to
the sound decency that is in him. He is not rotten, which most
young cultivated Englishmen are."[9] So convinced of Dikran's
decency was Lawrence that when he conceived a scheme to
start an utopian colony in Florida—thereby hoping to "bring
to pass a new earth and a new heaven"[10]—Lawrence invited
Dikran to join him. Eventually, however, Dikran's assertiveness
grew to annoy Lawrence; he complained, after a visit, that
his young friend refused to be "simple, fallible like other
mortals."[11] Michael Arlen was even more critical of himself
when he commented years later about the "somber, solitary,
and ambitious" youth he had been: "While longing to make
friends with men and women of intelligence, he was too conscious
that he approached them without charm but unaware that his
manner was without even dignity."[12]

Dikran, who longed for admittance to the fashionable world
he saw around him in London, dressed, even in his earliest
days, very elegantly—some said foppishly. (Nancy Cunard used
to refer to him, not without affection, as "The Baron."[13]) His
efforts sometimes met rebuffs which he seems to have felt keenly;

but such rejections served rather to sharpen than to discourage his ambitions. Once Dikran and a friend pooled their resources for a luncheon at Ciros, only to be turned down by the manager despite their protests that they were very important people. "One day," Dikran grumbled, "he will be only too glad to get me to lunch at Ciros, and I shall have a Rolls Royce bigger and better than any of these."[14] Later, when *The Green Hat* had made him rich, he bought a canary-yellow Rolls Royce that really was longer than anyone else's, and he had it registered in Manchester so that the license plate bore the initials M. A.

II *The Polemicist Manqué*

But such future events were unforeseen in those early years; for Dikran Kouyoumdjian was merely an obscure young man with curiosity, drive, and, of course, talent who needed an outlet and subject matter for his writing. He found both in the magazine *Ararat: A Searchlight on Armenia*, which was published by the Armenian United Association of London, which had offices at 47a, Redcliffe Square, South Kensington. Dikran, who until 1916 lived in a third-floor flat at 46 Redcliffe Road, just three streets away, joined the magazine as an editor and writer and helped present the case for Armenia before the English-speaking public.

Because of cultural and religious differences—the Armenians were Christians in an area ruled politically and dominated culturally by Moslems—Armenians had found themselves often in conflict with the Turkish majority, especially after 1885. By 1908, when the Young Turks overthrew the decrepit regime of Sultan Abdul Hamid II, the Armenians and other minorities hoped for tolerance and for a constitutional government; but, within a short time, these hopes were destroyed by a renewed outburst of chauvinism and serious harassment. When Turkey was humiliated in the Balkan Wars in 1912 and lost Macedonia, she was flooded with Mohammedan refugees. At that point, while allied with Germany in World War I, the Turkish government turned on the Armenians in earnest. In 1915 brutal "deportations" began. Community leaders were murdered, and forced marches of masses of people through hostile territory were conducted,

marches survived by only a small percentage. In the years that
followed, Armenians found themselves scattered around the
globe.[15] Those, like Dikran Kouyoumdjian, who were fortunate
enough to be secure and articulate were expected by their
compatriots to use their talents to arouse interest in their plight.

In the July, 1916, issue of *Ararat* Dikran Kouyoumdjian recorded his thoughts about being Armenian in an article—apparently his first signed publication—entitled "An Appeal to
Sense." He felt it was important to discredit the popular notion
of the "starving" Armenian and to replace it with a vision of
the *fighting* Armenian:

Most of the articles, pamphlets, and books I read of my countrymen
seem to encourage the casual person to think of the Armenian as
something like a beggar, with torn and tattered clothing, his eyes
red with weeping, his hands stretched out supplicating every passer-
by, a weak, helpless creature, without nationality, without self-
respect. A little of this is true; an Armenian in Armenia is a symbol
and a warning to all nations of the curse of nationality. Much of
it, if not untrue, is perverted truth. . . . An Armenian is not the weak,
helpless coward which his friends and enemies give you to imagine.
. . . He has in his time been an extremely good, and as effective as
possible, guerilla fighter, bandit, and rebel, and since he has been
more or less actively disliking his enemies for the last twenty-five
centuries, he is the father of all patriots, rebels and exiles.[16]

Tough talk, but the magazine had in general a tough, nationalistic
tone; and it quoted frequently such authors as the American
Abolitionist John Brown on the duty of the oppressed to revolt
against the oppressor. Many Armenians had died, and many
thousands were yet to die; indeed, high morale, pride, and
commitment were demanded of those who meant to take an
active role in the defense of their people.

In the August, 1916, issue, in the essay "The Young Armenian,"
Dikran expressed great disgust with his generation: its members
were unimaginative; they were too discreet, ordinary, and practical; but, worst of all, their "main aim in life would appear
to be, if not actually to hide their Armenianism, to keep the
knowledge to themselves as long as they can." Nationality is a
curse, he admitted, but "we may try as hard as we like to be

English or Fijian or whatever happens to attract us most—but we are Armenians."[17] In the September, 1916, issue he hammers at the same theme. "Until the instinct to hide goes from us, it is difficult to see how we can ever hope to be respected," he writes in the essay "The Very Serious Armenian."

But he ends with a curious paragraph in which he wonders whether it is worthwhile to criticize his countrymen in this way, for he doubts if they will either appreciate or heed advice. The modern Armenian's view of literature, he complains, is that "people scribble to earn a living while it can be done so much better in a shipping office. . . . Armenians will certainly not get a writer who can rouse the world to an interest in them till they begin to deserve one by wanting one."[18] Despite his own doubts, the budding author assumes an offensive position: he is willing to mount the podium, but where is his audience? What is to be done for a people who would rather encourage good business than good writing? With these questions, the division between Dikran Kouyoumdjian and his past was expressed.

In *The London Venture* Arlen describes a conversation in which the division was widened to a breach. When an artist whom he visits chides him for being unadventurous, unimaginative, lazy, and trivial, Dikran answers that he intends to "adventure" many things—"but not sensationally, you know. I mean, I can't look at myself straight, I can only look at myself sideways."

And when I write a novel—for of course I will write one, since England expects every young man to write a novel—the quality I shall desire in it will be, well, fastidiousness. . . . I come from the East; I shall go to the East; I shall try to strike the literary mean between the East and the West in me—between my Eastern mind and Western understanding. It will be a great adventure.

"The East is a shambles," he said shortly. And in that sentence lay my own condemnation of my real self; if any hope of fame ever lay in me, I suddenly realised, it was in that acquired self which had been to a public school and thought it not well bred to have too aggressive a point of view.[19]

Obviously his period of writing simple polemics was over; he could not conduct himself in a "fastidious," unaggressive manner

when responding to attempted genocide. But, just as obviously,
Dikran understood he was abandoning some part of his "real" self.

III   *From Polemic to Romance*

During the years 1915 and 1916, Dikran frequented the Bomb
Shop, a bookstore run by a genial father and son, George and
Frank Henderson, who used to let him and his friends borrow
great numbers of books. Author and translator Paul Selver writes
of coming to know the group and, because they lived not far
apart, of spending many evenings walking home with Dikran
after dinner at the Café Royal on Regent Street. Deciding
Dikran was an interesting man, Selver introduced him to Alfred
R. Orage and thus helped him to reach a wider, non-Armenian
audience and to receive sound advice about his writing.[20]

Orage, an economist, an editor, and the patron of young
writers, published a weekly called *The New Age*, which was
subsidized by the Fabians. A strong but undogmatic Socialist,
he had wide interests and sympathies; and the editorial office
of *The New Age* was a convenient place to congregate and to
meet such contributors as George Bernard Shaw, H. G. Wells,
G. K. Chesterton, Hilaire Belloc, Havelock Ellis, and Arnold
Bennett—or younger writers to whom Orage lent encouragement,
like Katherine Mansfield, Richard Aldington, Ezra Pound, and
Herbert Read. Arlen describes the office and Orage, as the
publisher Horton, in *The Green Hat*.

In 1913 the Orientalist Marmaduke Pickthall, known today
for his translation of *The Koran*, began a series in *The New Age*
in praise of the Moslem religion and Turkey which was later
published as the book *With The Turk in War-Time*. "The Turk,"
he wrote in a later but typically rhapsodic passage, "is thinking
all the time of such essential matters as the origin of life, its
transiency, the meaning and worth of human love, the ordeal
of death. His life is beautiful with this poetic earnestness."[21]
Perhaps as a counterbalance to such commendatory views, Orage,
who enjoyed setting his contributors at each other's throats,
republished Dikran's *Ararat* article "An Appeal to Sense" in
the August 3, 1916, issue of *The New Age*.

In the weeks that followed, Dikran submitted a variety of

pieces: mediocre attempts at informal essays; book reviews; short plays; and, more interesting, a continuing series that might have been titled "A Young Armenian Works Out His Identity Problem in Public"—articles which allow us to trace the steps by which Dikran Kouyoumdjian found his way to the style and subject matter that were to make him famous. At the same time, a view of the turmoil of his inner life is seen in an essay called "The Function of Daggers," which appeared in *The New Age* of January 11, 1917. Trying to think of a present to take to a friend, Dikran decides on a knife that had belonged to his father. No toy, it was a real knife that he had been forbidden as a child to play with. Looking at it, he recalls the passions of his ancestors and a story he had heard of an Armenian who had assassinated a tyrannical Russian viceroy. Later, while walking to his friend's house, he is bumped rudely by a stranger. Hard put to control his fury, he finds his fingers on the handle of the dagger: "O to have been able to raise the unsheathed blade and plunge it deep into the fleshiness of that brute! I can feel it now—the sickly pain of reason resisting that natural impulse, conquering it, pushing me past that man, so near to death as he never was, causing me, a few steps further, to look back on that one wracking second with a thankful jeer at myself."[22] Although we would be mistaken if we leaned too heavily on the anecdote, it does reveal how near to the surface the passions of this fastidious man could be.

Dikran's literary mentors advised him about his future. Orage, who had suggested that Katherine Mansfield adopt a realistic, natural manner, stressed that Dikran, an uprooted Armenian and a cosmopolitan, should develop an artificial, cleverly wrought style.[23] Moreover, D. H. Lawrence and George Moore also told him that he was by nature a romantic writer. From a commercial viewpoint, this advice was superb; for the artificial style and his romantic subjects created a market for him.

On August 9, 1917, a piece appeared titled "Michael Arlen: A Fragment of a Novel." In it, Dikran used for the first time the name he was to take legally as his own. The hero of this curious work is a writer who dies in utmost poverty, a "strange, unattached" young man, "an artist ... whose pent-up, over-fastidious aestheticism had no other effect than to make of him a monk without a monastery." A solitary, gallant figure, he believes in nothing; but he spends his undisciplined life searching for beauty, though with declining creativity. "Arlen" is contrasted with Ben, a simple caretaker of deep religious faith who is completely at home and content in this world. As "Michael Arlen" lies dying, the youth comments with relief that the process is "sanitary."[24]

The temptation to interpret such a work in terms of its author's life is difficult to resist, and the question arises as to whom Dikran was "killing off" in this story. Was he projecting a potential turn which his life might take if he let certain aspects of his character gain ascendancy? He feared his rootlessness and solitude and the decay of creative powers; he saw danger in allowing what was within him to become "pent-up" and find no release. When he invented an identity for himself, he repudiated "aestheticism" along with his poverty. The fictional Michael Arlen struggled honorably but lost; the living writer who later took his name lusted for success, fame and good company—and found them all, in abundance.

On August 15, 1918, the first of a series called "London Papers" appeared in *The New Age*. In them Dikran wrote subjectively of his schooldays, his early life in London, his enthusiasms and hopes, and his friends. The style is pleasant and ingratiating; and the book remains a valid self-portrait of a young man's growth. The articles were begun as imitations and/or parodies of George Moore, but Orage, who liked them, found them of value in their own right: "This is your best stuff,"[25] he said. And, as the series progressed, reader interest grew, especially in the lovely Shelmerdene, with whom the narrator has several intimate conversations about her past romances. She became the first of the "charming people" who were to delight so many readers.

With the advice and encouragement of friends (many claim credit for it), Dikran approached William Heinemann, who published the "London Papers" series in book form under the title *The London Venture*. However, Heinemann first advised Dikran Kouyoumdjian to find a name for himself that a bookseller could pronounce. Did he struggle with himself before doing so? Probably not. He apparently felt quite sincerely that it might make the difference between success and failure. "In changing my name," he said, "I have, I hope, robbed my readers of their last excuse for my obscurity."[26] He had; *The London Venture* launched his career.

CHAPTER 2

A Young Man's London

I The London Venture

The London Venture (1920), as a book, is unified more by a sensibility than by literary form. The narrator, who sits in a "strange library" in Northern England in the month of November, is temporarily tired of London, to which he hopes to return in the spring. He introduces himself through a series of loosely connected reminiscences about D. H. Lawrence, about the social side of London literary life, about the predicament of an alien alone in a great city, and about the dilemmas faced by a young man who decides to be independent. The self-portrait is intimate enough to seem revealing, and it is objective enough to elicit confidence in his observations. But other characters soon enter the story: Phyllis, "for whom his passion had died" and whom he had planned to write about in a novel; a girl whom he had met briefly at a bridge party and who had appeared six months later at his door, unannounced, one romantic evening, but who had finally married a "nice fat baronet"; Nikolay, an artist friend with whom he has a conversation about the relative merits of East and West as ways of life; Louis, a school friend with whom he founds a "society for Well Mannered People" and who dies in World War I. The characters are interesting enough, but the reader's concern is less with them than with the narrator's responses to them.

The heroine Shelmerdene, mentioned occasionally in the opening chapters, eventually dominates the book. She is married; she devotes her life to misty, drawn-out love affairs; she has an elaborate but unorthodox code of behavior; and she fascinates the narrator, who has suffered much from being in love with her, but who is destined to be no more than a friend. The last mention of Shelmerdene places her in Egypt, where she is happily "worshipping Ishtar"—that is, having a successful love affair after years of searching.

Two lengthy Shelmerdene sections are really short stories. In one episode Shelmerdene describes to the narrator an affair in which she is the pursuer of a man named Maurice. She fights for his love but loses; when he leaves her to take a post in Africa, he explains that he is incapable of a sustained relationship. She pines for months, but eventually, to expunge his memory, she goes with another man to the inn where she and Maurice had spent a romantic ten days. As she sits dining, Maurice appears in the doorway, sees her with her new lover, and disappears. He had returned from Africa; she had missed the cable that had asked her to meet him there: "And so, you see, I had won and lost and won again, but how pathetically.... Am I such a bad woman, d'you think?" (117). Shelmerdene is a character created to have frustrating love affairs; for, as the narrator perceives her, she means well but is betrayed by her own romantic impulses.

The second story narrated by Shelmerdene returns to her youth when she was a headstrong, beautiful eighteen-year-old girl, and it attempts to explain her character. Placed in the care of an elderly French Marquis by her father, she finds herself respectful of his ways but bored. The Marquis, however, falls in love with her and asks her to marry him and inherit his great wealth after his death. Soon a young man enters her life, for whom she has no feeling, but she uses him as her agent against the confining force of the Marquis. A chase on horseback occurs one morning when the Marquis tries to catch the pair, who are enjoying a forbidden ride; finally, in a melodramatic conclusion, she drives the old man away with a whip. He dies in broken-hearted dignity shortly after this episode.

Despite the material about Shelmerdene, the book's most persistent theme is the isolation of the narrator, Dikran. He laments his lonely early years in London; he longs for a "background" and a sense of identity; he "couldn't bear the idea of going through life as just a complacent Armenian" (60). Moreover, his immersion in art and literature has changed him: "I see that my middle age will be crabbed and made solitary by my books, and that I shall never have the heart to leave them and

go to the East to see the land of my father Haik[1]" (23). Shelmerdene sounds a pessimistic and, in some ways, prophetic note
when she warns Dikran, "In spite of all your English airs, you
will always be a pathetic little stranger in a very strange land,
fumbling for the key" (144). But only one solution appears
suitable to the narrator: he will leave the East behind and rely
on his "acquired" self.

The creation of a new personality is not accomplished easily,
of course, but requires restraint and control; and Arlen's self-
conscious efforts to achieve these qualities are a kind of subtheme
in the book. He will, he says, agree with complaints about the
"monotonous routine of politeness," but he also observes that
without indulging that routine "men cannot live decently." He
is offended, as he leaves London, by the cinema posters with
their "crude portrayal of the indecent passions of tiresome
people" (12). He objects, in a conversation with Shelmerdene,
to people who would destroy conventions:

Such people make life unclean. They talk about being "natural," and
succeed only in being boorish; they think that the opposite of
"natural" is "artificial," but that is absurd, for why was the title
"gentlemen" invented if not for the man who could put a presentable
gloss on his primitive, "natural" instincts in polite company? There
must always be etiquette in life and love, and there is no friendship
or passion which can justify familiarity breaking down the barriers
which hide every man and every woman from the outside world. (45)

For this reason, Arlen admires Henry James, who showed men
"to be subtle creatures . . . with barriers of reserve and strange-
ness between each person" (47). As Shelmerdene sees it, her
story about the Marquis teaches the lesson of "restraint." But
restraint satisfied only one side of Arlen's nature; he also writes
admiringly of D. H. Lawrence for possessing "a mass of passionate strength, that of an angry man straining with his nerves
because he despises his hands" (22). And, though Arlen committed himself to a life of self-control, he left behind or denied
his "real" self, as he admits, when he embarked on his London
venture.

Arlen received only thirty pounds for *The London Venture*,

but some of the "right" people began to talk about him because of it. According to Alec Waugh, many were of the opinion that Arlen and Kouyoumdjian were both pseudonyms for George Moore.[2] The *New York Times* reviewer described *The London Venture* as "an interesting and always original little volume" that "narrowly escapes brilliance."[3] F. Scott Fitzgerald was so impressed that he wrote to Maxwell Perkins: "a profound bow to my successor, Arlen—when I read *The London Venture* I knew he was a comer."[4] Fitzgerald later treated Ernest Hemingway to a recital one afternoon of the plots of all of Arlen's books. "He gave me sort of an oral Ph.D. thesis on Michael Arlen,"[5] Hemingway recalled.

The publication of *The London Venture* did involve one lapse from proper ethics: no mention was made that the materials had first appeared in *The New Age*. Perhaps Arlen thought the book would sell better if he neglected to mention that fact: Orage had great prestige among left-wing intellectuals, but, being a man of decided opinions, he had also acquired some enemies. Later, Arlen apologized in *The Green Hat* for his omission when the narrator describes a publisher named Horton and his magazine *The New Voice* and remarks that many authors had come to fame through Horton's patronage and then, after quarreling with the editor, "revenged themselves by republishing their *New Voice* stuff in book form and omitting to mention the *New Voice* as the first medium of publication." That, he asserts, "was discourteous of them."[6] In later years, Arlen did more to redeem himself; for, when Orage tried to revive *The New Age*, he wrote to his now successful former authors asking for financial help. Only Richard Aldington and Michael Arlen replied—Arlen, Orage told Aldington, with a "very generous check indeed."[7]

When *The London Venture* was reissued in paperback form in 1968 with an introduction by Sir Noel Coward, he wrote: "On re-reading *The London Venture* I have been enchanted all over again with the unforced wittiness of Dikran's writings and the individual elegance of his style. His affectionate evocation of the various aspects of London in the early Twenties seems to me, a possibly prejudiced observer, to be remarkably undated. ... His use of the English language too, vivid, colloquial and only very rarely a trifle tentative, has surely never received the

attention it deserves."[8] Like Coward, new readers to whose
attention the book has been brought by this edition have not
been disappointed.

II *"Piracy"*

Arlen's first novel, *"Piracy"* (1922), tells, through its hero, "the
history of England, two loves, and an ideal" (23). Ivor Marlay
loves two women of thirty: one when he is twenty-three; the
other, when he also is thirty; a third woman, who represents the
"ideal," appears in the closing chapters under bizarre circumstances. The book is in large measure a roman à clef; a "half
[of] London society"[9] figures in its pages; but *"Piracy"*—the
quotation marks are part of the title—is a young man's novel
and shows it. The style sometimes overwhelms the relatively
slight action, and Arlen often lavishes detail on thematically
irrelevant matters. The ending, preposterous and a bit desperate
in its reaching for conclusions on any terms, is either a ruinous
error or a joke. But the writing, where it works, flows very well;
and the characters are well observed, if not always understood
fully by the author.

Ivor Marlay, the illegitimate son of a nobleman—the product
of what his aunt calls "a beautiful love affair"—grows up well
provided for but, after his parents' death, isolated. Because of
his restlessness and his boredom with routine, he is expelled
from school for practical joking. His advisors, an aunt and an
uncle, urge him to develop a sense of purpose and encourage
him to accomplish something, besides being the custodian of
his wealth. In response, Ivor becomes an author who publishes
novels with such titles as *Fair Ladies of London* and *The Legend
of the Last Courtesan*; and he makes his way into London's
social life.

Marlay's first "love" is Magdalen Gray, whose husband explores
Asia while "she explores everything else" (76); and their affair
lasts through 1913 and part of 1914. Of Magdalen Gray, a "woman
of quality," a hostile acquaintance says, "'that woman . . . burns
whatever she touches" (137); but, though Ivor stops writing
while in love with her, he does learn, through her influence, about
people and about himself: "She polished him, and she smoothed

down the sharp dogmatisms and conceits which had so far taken the place of conversation with him" (109). At twenty-three, Ivor is a serious and constant lover; he fails to understand not only the temporary nature of the relationship but also Magdalen Gray's objections to his faithfulness. " 'There's a fatality about my kind of love,' Magdalen said, softly, miserably, heroically. 'It ends. . . . Women have moods' " (116). When Ivor becomes ill with influenza, Magdalen leaves the country during his convalescence: "She hated a mess. She would have made a wonderful playwright—if plays consisted only of exits" (141).

When Ivor goes to war in 1916 Arlen strives to describe the England of those times, to indicate what it lost, and to recall the "new and vivid charm" of the prewar generation:

They were so immediately likeable, so fine! A new kind of young men they were entirely, these few from the Universities, and much less "provincial" than new young men had ever been before. . . . In everything they were a denial of their fathers, for these young men were sceptical of generalisations: in everything they were a denial of the catchwords for which they were to fight; and in everything they were the finest expression of the paralytic civilisation for which they were to die. Vulgarity of thought was to them the abomination of abominations; and they died because of it. They were to go out to fight in a war for chivalry, and they were to die in a morass of spite. (81–82)

Ivor matures through his relationship with Magdalen Gray; through his experiences during the war, in which valued friends die; and through the pain of his wounds when he loses an arm in the fighting.

Ivor's second love is Virginia Tracy, who plays a minor role in the first half of the novel as one of the young ladies in Ivor's social group. Wed first to an American who turned out to be a cocaine-addicted homosexual, she later marries George Tarlyon, a charming, witty, cynical, and, eventually, unfaithful scoundrel; and the affair between Ivor and Virginia begins when Tarlyon too blatantly flaunts a new mistress before her. Ivor's new affair is intense and deep; but again the woman tires of it. Ivor demands that they marry: "I'm not philandering with you, I'd have you know. I have finished with philandering" (229). But to Virginia, the idea of Ivor as a husband is impossible: "You simply don't look or think or talk like any possible husband; it's perfectly obvious to the meanest intelligence that you are a lover and always will be. You simply aren't casual enough to be anything else, Ivor" (229). To Ivor, however, marriage is "just a matter of orderliness" and "one must simply be a responsible person, even a lover must be a responsible person, if he is to get any work done" (230). And work is the key to his problem: when he is with Virginia, he neither writes nor develops. As Virginia describes his situation, "This love has been stronger than you, and you are going soft and rotten with it—you are drifting with me, my sweet, instead of my striving with you!" (251).

When Virginia falls ill and requires a difficult operation, Ivor remains with her; but the relationship changes. When George Tarlyon reenters her life, Ivor and Virginia quarrel; and Ivor leaves London. She sends two telegrams asking him to return; but, out of hurt pride, he delays. Weakened by her operation, Virginia dies before Ivor sees her again.

Magdalen and Virginia—whose contrasting names have less symbolic significance than they should—cannot fulfill Ivor's needs. Both, to be sure, have glamor—a potent and mysterious force in Arlen's world:

Glamour! Now this glamour is a very remarkable thing, a strange and indefinable thing, and very rare: for it does not fall on women because they have many lovers, it does not fall on women because they are wonderfully constant to one lover, and it certainly does not fall on women who Do Things. Sometimes it happens on a courtesan, sometimes on a great lady; but this glamour is no snob, it cares nothing for the claims of fashion, for it may quite well happen on a dairymaid, so that a whole countryside grows aware of her and a whole country sorrows for her death. . . . Yes, this glamour is a wayward thing, it just comes and touches a lovely woman in each generation, and because of it her youth is long remembered and her middle-age forgiven. (158–59)

But "rottenness" also exists in glamor and often tragedy is its fate; and for all his attraction to glamor, Ivor needs something more earthy and substantial.

At the end of the novel, he gets what he has been seeking. It is May 1, 1921; Ivor, distressed and bitter, sits alone in the Mont Agel Restaurant brooding about his life. He finally rouses himself and, while walking the streets, meets a lady standing in a doorway who wears an expensive Chinchilla coat. Confused and curiously innocent, she asks Ivor—seemingly a safe escort because of his missing arm—to take her home. He recognizes her as "Pamela Star," subject of a portrait by Augustus John which had created a stir when it was displayed in 1916. She had become a mystery woman, a legend. Now, in a most bizarre touch, Pamela Star takes Ivor home and shows him the corpse of Aram Melekian, Armenian multimillionaire, who has died just that evening. Pamela, originally Pam Snagg and a plumber's daughter, was Melekian's ward, then mistress, finally his companion, and now his heir.

Now the richest woman in the world, Pamela is confused without her former protector; in Ivor, she finds a new protector and a true lover. As they walk out of the house into the dawn, Ivor cries, "Our way is obvious! . . . Romance must plant its feet firmly on reality, for it's life that makes us beautiful, not we that beautify life. So we will acknowledge our debt to life by walking up the ugly Edgeware Road rather than towards the fat and horrid squares of Bayswater. Why, Pamela Star, anything might happen up the Edgeware Road—even Cricklewood might happen, the legendary source of Bus 16!" (324). When Ivor later leaves Pamela at her door, she tells the boy delivering milk: "I had an image without a face . . . until that man came and put a face to it" (327).

On a realistic level, the ending is absurd; and it is apparent that, despite the frequent mentions of precise locations in London and thinly veiled portraits of familiar figures, Arlen's intention is to develop an abstract scheme; for, as has been noted, he stated that the story of Ivor was to be "the history of England, two loves, and an ideal." The "ideal" contains contradictory elements: on the one hand it is an urge to be "up and doing things," to be engaged in "fine endeavor" (171). Ivor's Aunt Moira urged him, "For Heaven's sake, Ivor, don't be slack, don't be sodden! You must think Something, do Something!" (172). On the other hand, the ideal was to be embodied in a perfect woman, "a woman worth living for and dying with"; for, as Ivor says, "One wants the love and constancy of a dairymaid and the lust and pride and wit of a great lady" (74). When Ivor is provided with the mysterious, beautiful, fabulously wealthy plumber's daughter, he has a share of the world's aristocratic glamor and at the same time satisfies his middle-class need for something solid and dependable.

Arlen characteristically, here as elsewhere, begins with real people, situations, and events. In his Englishness, in his birth, in his war experiences, and in his wounds Ivor is quite unlike Arlen, of course; but Arlen teases his readers by mentioning as early works of Ivor's *The Decline of Humour* and *The Function of Daggers*—the titles of essays that Arlen had written as Dikran Kouyoumdjian for *The New Age*. The "casual, fearless, handsome Lord Tarlyon" (86) has been identified with Napier Stuart, Lord Alington,[10] whose devastating charm was described in terms like Arlen's by one of his admirers, Tallulah Bankhead, in her autobiography.[11] Virginia seems in some details patterned after Nancy Cunard: Virginia's mother is named Lady Carnal, and her two carefully tended curls, nicknamed "Swan and Edgar" after the London department store, recall Nancy Cunard's characteristic "beavers," described by her biographer as "curving over her cheekbones like twin scimitars."[12] Aram Melekian has a counterpart in Calouste Gulbenkian, who acquired the name "Mr. Five Percent" because he had gained, through manipulation, that share of the enormous Middle Eastern oil profits.[13]

Aram Melekian provides Arlen with the occasion for a disquisition in his new, ironic manner on Armenians: Melekian "was the only proud gesture that wretched race has ever made since Jesus died to save the souls of men. . . . A wise old man, Sir Aram Melekian, but bitter. . . . He had financed several little wars, and it was known that with the great Greek millionaire, he had helped the Allies considerably in the last war—his idea being, some people said, that since England and France had befriended Armenia almost out of existence he was only too pleased to do what he could for them." Most curious is the question of Sir Aram's nose, "which was what's called a decidedly Jewish-looking affair; whereas though Armenians have frequently been described as very Jewish-looking, the truth of the matter is that Jews are very Armenian-looking, for the Armenians are the senior race and have, therefore, a prior right to that nose which the Jews, perhaps rather indiscreetly, have always claimed as their own" (314–15). Arlen's ironic chauvinism demonstrates how far he has come from his days of earnest polemics.

The reaction to "*Piracy*" was generally favorable. Arlen's American publisher, George Doran, thought it one of Arlen's "major achievements."[14] The reviewer for the *Spectator* found the book "queerly dissatisfying and irritating"; Pamela and Marlay, he complained, are "incomplete"; the novel has no unity; "and yet," he adds, "it must be spoken of respectfully" and its author, "if he can learn precision . . . may . . . be a great novelist."[15] The *New York Times* found the work "delicate" but "thin."[16] The *Saturday Review* objected more strongly: "Mr. Arlen does, incredibly, but actually, think that there is something splendid and romantic—*something interesting*—in a world of wicked wanton women and splendid sardonic men. . . . It is all so young, so artless! Let Mr. Arlen ask himself, only once, what he would think of people who talked in life, as he makes everybody talk in his novel!"[17] But, of course, objections about such "wicked wanton women" sell more books than any amount of tepid praise.

A final, rather rueful footnote to the story of "*Piracy*" was provided by the late Bennett Cerf. He and Beatrice Kaufman, he recalls, "turned down Michael Arlen's "*Piracy*" when it was submitted to Boni and Liveright in the early 1920s. Both she and I thought it was a poor book indeed. This decision came back to haunt us, of course, when his book of stories . . . *These Charming People* was published elsewhere and made a hit, and when *The Green Hat* swept the country, we were particularly mortified."[18]

CHAPTER 3

Short Stories: 1920-1925

BETWEEN 1920 and 1925 Michael Arlen published the collection *The London Venture*, the two novels *"Piracy"* and *The Green Hat*, and over forty short stories, most of which were collected in three volumes: *The Romantic Lady* (1921), *These Charming People* (1923), and *May Fair* (1925). To populate his fictional world Arlen created a repertory company of lively characters. Shelmerdene appears often in the short stories, though more passively than in *The London Venture*; George Tarlyon, who is dangerously irresponsible in *"Piracy"*, is transformed in the short stories into an amiable man-about-town, a representative of a graceful carelessness that Arlen obviously found attractive. While some variety exists in the stories, the tone, characters, and the mode are very much of a single period and sensibility.

I *Tone and Technique*

These Charming People Arlen calls "a tapestry of the fortunes, follies, adventures, gallantries and general activities of Shelmerdene (that lovely lady), Lord Tarlyon, Mr. Michael Wagstaffe and some others of their friends of the lighter sort,"[1] a description which gives a reasonably good sense of the spirit of both books. In *May Fair*, Arlen introduces the narrator-persona Ralph Wyndham Trevor, who tells some of the stories; but the angle of narration is not rigid. *May Fair* is "an entertainment purported to reveal to gentlefolk the real state of affairs existing in the very heart of London during the fifteenth and sixteenth years of the reign of his Majesty King George the Fifth."[2] The operative word is, of course, "purported" and not "real." The absence of realism struck nearly all the reviewers and critics of Arlen's short stories. One reviewer spoke of his "witty, flippant, snobbish, dandyish disdain of the vulgarities of existence."[3] Another, who commented that Arlen "has never been as much concerned with plots and the glamour of his people as he has been with the business of putting one word after another," called him "primarily a writer, pure and simple, with the manufacture of stories and the creation of character, barring only Iris March, a secondary and inferior talent with him."[4]

Francis Melville Perry, in a book about writing which places Arlen with Henry James, Joseph Conrad, and Edgar Allan Poe as masters of fiction, suggests that Arlen's "imitation of 'models' instead of life, . . . his ironic treatment of emotion, his concern with manners rather than morals, his will to please rather than reform, his conception of pleasure as a product of wit rather than imagination, of literature as play for busy, keen minds, his obviously affected sentiment, his urbanity and sophistication, separate Arlen from the romantic writers and range him with a group of self-conscious clever modernists, who measure men by their wits and do not take life or letters too seriously."[5] Another reviewer, characterizing Arlen's stories as "cream puffs" but as perfect of their kind, suggested that, "if you wish corn beef and cabbage, you have no business to be reading Michael Arlen."[6]

The Michael Arlen of the early 1920s described himself as a romancer. *The Green Hat* is subtitled, "A Romance, For a Few People," and Arlen constantly reminds his readers in his early books that his creations are fanciful. He may have influenced a few real people to behave like his characters, but his fictional Mayfair is as imaginary as Rudolph Friml's Balkans.[7] Arlen's setting is a place "where motor-cars grow from the cracks in the pavement and ladies recline in slenderness on divans, playing with rosaries of black pearls and eating scented macaroons out of bowls of white jade."[8] The term *romance* has many meanings, but always it involves a commitment to the imaginative rather than to the familiar; for Arlen, the term meant that he wrote about his audience's latest desires and aspirations as its members understood them. This view needs to be emphasized because there were some critics, unfamiliar with his materials, who regarded him otherwise. For example, his American publisher, George Doran, who thought *These Charming People* to be a "clinical study of social London," hailed Arlen as "one of the foremost realists of the day."[9]

In style as well as content Arlen emphasized the artificial. "I can't look at myself straight," he wrote in *The London Venture*; "I can only look at myself sideways" (84). He might also have been speaking of his subjects, for he viewed them from many angles until he found the one that provided the best opportunities for embellishment. In "The Romantic Lady," the narrator, sitting still as he is told a story, thinks of how Joseph Conrad's "gentle Marlow . . . transfixed his hearers as he led them inexorably through the labyrinth of Lord Jim's career."[10] "The Romance of Iris Poole," which relies for its effects on a series of nonchronological revelations, begins with a commentary on style which tells us something about Arlen's methods: "It is only the trained artificiality of writers—their technique, so to say—that enables them to begin their tales from a certain point and go directly to a certain ending. . . . The tales that are spun from life cannot be complacently fitted along a straight line of narration, but incline to zigzag unaccountably from one point of memory to another; until the tale is fulfilled, or rather, fulfils itself by these deft and disordered touches of the realism of memory."[11] "He did not so much tell a story as embroider one,"[12] Alec Waugh commented; but sometimes Arlen's story disappears and all that is left is the embroidery. That Arlen could make such writing successful, however, is a tribute to his technique.

In commenting on his own writing, Arlen could be thoroughly unsentimental. To an interviewer in 1925 he said, "If you want to know what I think I'm doing in my books, I think I'm telling a story. If I do my job well, I think the story's all right. It's all very simple—either you tell a story or you don't." In the same interview he described O. Henry as "the master technician of the short story" who, trick endings and all, manages to convince his reader "of the relentless logic of what he's had to relate."[13] In a semiautobiographical short story first published in 1929, Arlen pictures himself as telling an artistic, sophisticated young lady:

Bad or good writer, I'm a born writer. It's as natural for me to make a living out of writing as it is for a plumber out of plumbing. And a born writer, a man like me, writes anything that comes to his hand.

... He doesn't hang around with a lot of conceited and confused ideas in his head about the regeneration of art, he doesn't think a short story must follow Tchekov's [*sic*] model or a novel some other fellow's, he just writes anything he is offered money for—stories, essays, serials, novels, plays—in fact, he is a professional. But by the way you people talk of writing, my dear Priscilla, anyone might think writing was something unusual and lofty, giving a man the right to think he is something apart, but actually it's just an ordinary profession.[14]

By expressing such disdain for aesthetic considerations, Arlen anticipates some of his critics' complaints; and he also asserts his own practical sense of professionalism.

But while emphasizing the calculated and artificial elements in Arlen's writing, we should not ignore the possibilities of deeper purpose in his work during this period. In a review of *These Charming People*, Edwin Bjorkman suggested such possibilities when he wrote of Arlen's literary purpose, which "must be held no less bitter in its earnestness because it is pursued in a spirit of jest so abandoned that at times it borders on ribaldry. At the core of this purpose I, for one, find an implacable hatred of all conventional humbug, . . . a sham-defying mockery that to me at least seems the best cure for the dominant ailment of the hour."[15] As we range through the stories a pattern of attitudes emerges which is, indeed, a commentary on life, manners, and morals, although it strenuously attempts to seem anything but that—an effect which is, of course, also a matter of style.

II *Charming Women*

The heroines of Arlen's short fiction are attractive, fashionable Londoners with Mayfair addresses. Though they are well off and independent in their social activities, their personal resources are "feminine" ones, and so their success in life depends on how well they can attract and manipulate the affections of men. Arlen's ideal woman has the capacity to "misbehave" sexually if she is not properly attended to, but basically she is a person of sensitivity, loyalty, beauty, and discretion. Arlen's "evil" women, on the other hand, lack restraint and suffer from excessive wantonness and cruelty. Arlen's audiences evidently found in his female characters a largely sympathetic explanation for tendencies they observed around them.

A good number of Arlen's stories are homilies that instruct men to pay closer attention to their women. In "A Romance in Old Brandy"[16] for example, an old man convinces a young friend not to divorce his somewhat giddy wife: "'She'll grow,' said Mr. Lapwing. . . . 'And, Valentine, she has got more right to be an ass than you have. Remember that. There's no use being sentimental about it, but they put up with a lot of pain, women.'" In "The Three-Cornered Moon,"[17] a wife takes revenge on her bored and divorce-minded husband by posing as her own twin sister, thereby causing him to fall in love with her again.

In "The Battle of Berkeley Square,"[18] George Tarlyon has an appendicitis attack on the same day that his sister Shirley is having a child. He dreams of being transported into Shirley's body as she delivers, and the experience teaches him that women are "marvelous . . . by reason of what they put up with in men one way and another." In "The Hunter After Wild Beasts,"[19] Aubrey Carlyle, who spends most of his time hunting wild game or distinguishing himself in warfare, believes he is happily married and is astonished when his wife leaves him with a simple note: "You know why, dear. Goodbye." But the point is that he doesn't, even after she comes back and explains: "You hunt wild beasts, don't you, Aubrey? . . . And when you come back from your hunting you ravage me like a wild beast . . . and then you go away again. . . . Oh, Aubrey, how you have sinned against love."

In "The Real Reason Shelmerdene Was Late for Dinner"[20] that "lovely lady," who is dressing for dinner with George Tarlyon, laments to her maid that she is now thirty-four years old. When she gets a phone call from her long-absent husband, who humbly asks her to dinner, Shelmerdene, despite her age, refuses. She will not dine with the man who years before had "suddenly, bitterly, vengefully left her life because, being a child, she had taken a silly notion to make him jealous– . . . It is not so easy as that."

"To Lamoir"[21] concerns a marriage which has failed because of human folly and the demands of daily life. The husband, Hugh, had dreamed as a child of meeting a young girl, an ideal playmate; they had climbed a tree and kissed, then parted never to meet again. The memory of her haunts him for years, however; and, when as an adult, he meets Lamoir, he is convinced she is the dream girl, though he knows she cannot be. They marry; but, as the years go by, he becomes deeply involved in his avocation of collecting fine objects. She leaves him after a time because, she says, she loves him too much to live through the ordinary years of marriage: "You see, I want to be free to love you, and you won't let me.... God has given me no children, Hugh. He has given me only my love for you. That is all I have, and I have been sacrificing it to you for ten years, but now I am growing afraid for it, it's become such a poor, beaten, wretched bit of thing, and so I must leave you." After nine years of separation, they are ready to see each other again; but, recalling his playmate fantasy, Hugh delays going to meet Lamoir in order to observe the anniversary of his youthful dream experience. He is found dead of a broken neck at the foot of a tree; Lamoir died the same day. Though mawkish, the story nevertheless advances the concept of the buried "ideal" which many of Arlen's characters clutch carefully and faithfully to themselves. In this case, Hugh's pursuit of his dream at the expense of reality is seen, somewhat ambiguously, as personal folly and as inescapable destiny.

Though sophisticated and aware, the women of these stories are not, in the feminist's sense, emancipated; they define themselves too much in terms of their men and of what those men permit them to be. They function best in roles for which their mates "intend" them, in the drawing room or in the boudoir, rather than in the world of male competitiveness. But men must treat their women more carefully than they do, Arlen suggests, or the results will be painful.

In other stories, Arlen cleverly reverses audience expectations to gain his effects. In "The Luck of Captain Fortune,"[22] Shelmerdene and Ralph Wyndham converse in a restaurant with a distressed man who tells a story about a clever woman with a taste for politics but without the intellectual capacity for a career. Despite her handicaps, she becomes one of the first women members of Parliament; but her success is due to the help of a selfless male friend who writes her speeches for her.

After her success, however, she abandons her friend to marry a much-decorated military hero, Captain Fortune. The "twist" ending reveals that the troubled narrator is not the abandoned friend, but Captain Fortune, who, thinking he had married a woman of talent, found himself attached to one who was no more than a beautiful ventriloquist's dummy: "'Of course,' he whispered, 'she has never been able to make a speech since. How could she? Without her old friend she is just a lovely woman...whose life centers around her care for Captain Fortune.'"

In contrast to the women of these stories, Arlen depicted another type: the voracious, depraved woman who has the power to trap and fascinate but lacks kindness and restraint. "Consuelo Brown"[23] concerns a girl of eighteen who betrays one young man and drives his brother to suicide. A girl with "lithe limbs and curling lips, laughing eyes and loose heart—a hungry girl, made to rot men" (177). Consuelo lacks the restraint and maturity that makes Shelmerdene human; she thereby represents the destructive element in Arlen's "fascinating" women.

In another story, "Consuelo,"[24] a man in the act of making love to his best friend's wife is nearly discovered when, as the two sit in a summer cabin in a garden, the husband approaches. The man is saved when a mysterious hand reaches through the window to hand him a cigar with a long ash—his proof of innocence. Twenty years later he finds the answer to the mystery: the hand and the fortuitous cigar had belonged to another man with whom Consuelo had also made an assignation but who had gallantly saved the day for the adulterers. This Consuelo, as the narrator describes her, "was neither a witch nor a whore, but [a woman] whose fault and misfortune simply lay in her having no anchor in any sort of code of respectability." After she has committed suicide, the narrator observes: "I can almost understand now...how she died as she did. Life on those lines must have got too complicated."

III *Gallant Men*

The male characters in Arlen's short stories are drawn from a limited range of types. Many "Establishment" figures are to be found among them, men of social standing whose main concern is with manners and proper modes of behavior. They are, to be sure, figures of Romance, but they embody attitudes and codes from which we can form a conception of proper male behavior. In this respect, courtesy between males in matters of love provides a theme for several stories. In "The Irreproachable Conduct of a Gentleman Who Refused a Knighthood,"[25] Cyrus Fall tells George Tarlyon of his romantic dilemma: Fall is in love with the widow of an army friend but is having no success because she is devoted to her husband's memory. Fall explains that he knows the husband had been, in fact, unfaithful and undeserving; but his sense of honor prevents him from using the information to win her. Later, Tarlyon calls the woman and insults her terribly—and, seemingly, gratuitously. The woman, it emerges, was in love with Tarlyon and had hoped he would marry her; and she had merely been "palming off that ghastly lie... about a husband she had never cared a damn about." In the end, she marries Cyrus Fall, who then reveals to Tarlyon that he had known of her infatuation all along: "That is why I told you of my dilemma that night—after which, as a man of honor, you could do but one thing, since my intentions were serious and yours were not."

Adept as he is at depicting such romantic maneuvering among the socially prominent, Arlen seems to prefer male characters who are just on the other side of the law. They are men without means, but with surprisingly strong standards of behavior, and as a result they find themselves in conflict with both the laws and the hypocrisies of organized society. "The Ace of Cads"[26] deals with the noble deception practiced by the dashing "Beau" Maturin, "a very St. George for looks and as lost for grace as the wickedest imp in hell." He is summoned to the home of Sir Guy de Gramercy, "a *seigneur* of a past century who made no secret of the fact that he disdained any part in this [century]." Sir Guy's young granddaughter has fallen in love with the penniless, forty-seven-year-old Beau; and Sir Guy hopes to bribe him to break off the match. Surprisingly, Beau agrees. His method is to tell a discreditable story about himself in the presence of Sir Guy's widowed daughter-in-law, Eleanour, and his granddaughter, Joan. Beau says he had, years before, seduced the

fiancée of a young friend, and he had been aided in doing so
by money he had borrowed from the same friend. The granddaughter, who could not be forced to give up Beau, voluntarily
rejects him after hearing the story. The "twist" ending reveals
that Beau had told the story incorrectly: Sir Guy's daughter-in-law
reveals that she was the girl of the story, Beau was the young
man in love, and Sir Guy's dead son was the dishonorable friend.
Beau keeps the bribe; for, as he tells Sir Guy, "Your house
owes it to me."

Two ways of life collide—or seem to collide—in this story.
Sir Guy is the voice of an older generation that is convinced of
the dignity and rightness of its ways. Possessing a family name
and a fortune, Sir Guy regards both as "a responsibility rather
than as a means for self-indulgence" and as of no value "without
the dignity of some office and the ardor of some responsibility."
Beau, as Sir Guy perceives him, is an incredible man to whom
such ancient words as "honor," "loyalty," and "betrayal" are without meaning. Beau admits he enjoys money, and he gambles
it away carelessly. But for Sir Guy's ancient military record, un-
specified but apparently gained in the service of the Empire,
Beau has no respect because of his own experience in World
War I: "One didn't need the stimulous of alcohol to turn
machine-guns on to a lot of septic-looking niggers without even
a water pistol between them . . . but the Germans needed fighting,"
he says, partly to explain his dissolute life. But, despite his
seeming disrespect for Sir Guy's world, Beau is really quite
conservative. He is uncomfortable before Sir Guy's pleading,
for he is offended "as much to see pride humbled and the
mighty fallen as to watch the lowly being exalted and the
humble getting above themselves." Beau, although not young
himself, attracted the young because of his unspoiled inde-
pendence and his preference for a life of daring; but he finally
proves to be as determined to uphold conventions—some conventions, anyway—as does Sir Guy.

IV   *The Cavalier of the Streets*

Arlen had good fun with stories of an outlaw who calls himself
the "Cavalier of the Streets" and who makes his profession the

robbing of the rich and pampered while he lives by a self-imposed code of conduct suitable to the moral fringes of society. In the first and best of these stories, "The Man with the Broken Nose,"[27] George Tarlyon and Ralph Wyndham Trevor meet a strange, dark man at the National Gallery who announces himself as a Zeytounli: " 'Zeytoun,' he said, 'is a fortress in Armenia. For five hundred years Zeytoun has not laid down her arms, but now she is burnt stones on the ground. The Zeytoulis, sir, are the hill-men of Armenia. I am an Armenian.' " He rejects their pity because "by sticking to it year in and year out for five hundred years, Armenians have in a tactful way slain more Turks than Turks have slain Armenians. That is why I am so proud of being Armenian." Tarlyon and Trevor believe his story because "'no one would say he was Armenian if he wasn't, would he?'"

When they meet him again in Grosvenor Square, the strange man explains that he is about to assassinate Achmed Jzzit Pasha, the "Young Turk," who has kidnapped his sister Anais and intends to put her in his harem. The two Englishmen, who prevail on him to forget the murder and to settle for the freeing of his sister, promise to aid him. Entering the house with him, they hold down the furious Achmed while the Zeytounli searches for his sister. But he never returns, and the "Turk" turns out to be his father, a Mr. Wagstaffe. The son, Michael, has stolen his father's valuable coin collection and George Tarlyon's Rolls Royce. Mr. Wagstaffe explains: "He's a clever boy, Michael. . . . He is always on the lookout for what he calls the Mugs. . . . He calls himself the cavalier of the streets, but when he is up to any of his tricks he disguises himself as an Armenian—the disguise consisting merely of his saying he is an Armenian. It's so simple, he says, for the Mugs believe him at once, on the ground that no one would say he was an Armenian if he wasn't." There really was a Zeytoun that remained unconquered for centuries and though this story is a rather loose way to proclaim such an accomplishment, Arlen makes a vivid tale of it.

In "The Cavalier of the Streets,"[28] Fay Avalon, beautiful and charming, is, at thirty-eight, "older than most women"; and she finds romance in an affair with a counterfeit prince, a refugee from the Russian Revolution who makes a poor living as a bad artist. She is soon accosted in the street by a shabby young

man who threatens to inform her husband. The blackmailer is
Michael Wagstaffe, Cavalier of the Streets; but he is also a
gentleman—"a gentleman . . . is a man who is never *unintentionally*
rude to anyone"—and he soon finds himself sympathizing with
his victim; indeed, he is in love with her. He finds a way, then,
of making her aware that the "Prince" is really the blackmailer:
" 'That,' he said harshly, 'will teach a lovely lady to love scum.
. . . I have sinned against you . . . but you have done worse. You
have sinned against yourself!' " Fay Avalon is impressed; but,
before she can shift her affections, Wagstaffe has disappeared.

In "Salute the Cavalier,"[29] Michael Wagstaffe crashes a party
given by Mr. and Mrs. Felix Waite; and, being a suspicious-
looking character, he is detained by the police when a diamond
is stolen from the hostess. When no evidence of his guilt is
found, he is released; and he goes immediately to the home of
a girl he had observed leaving the party. Betty, a flower girl
whom he had seduced while at Oxford, later came to London
and nearly married Felix Waite. Michael Wagstaffe guesses,
correctly, that she is the thief; and he is determined to share the
booty so that he can leave England. He is surprised, however,
when she reveals her motive: she is not planning to sell the
diamond but to keep it as a memento of her near-marriage to
Waite. When the police, who have followed Michael, arrive, he,
in a romantic gesture, takes the blame for the robbery: " 'Good
night, pretty Betty,' called the cavalier of the streets. 'I'm sorry
about the wrong I did you at Oxford. But I'll do you a good
turn one day. . . .' "

These stories are obviously written as entertainments, but we
are led to suspect that the Cavalier, an outsider who must work
on the fringes of society, but whose desperate circumstances
mask a fastidious sensibility, gains some of his charm and
energy through being a romantic projection of his author's own
sense of alienation.

V *Ghost Stories and Surprise Endings*

Arlen often used supernatural themes, and his stories regularly
appear in anthologies of ghost and horror tales. He could also,
however, fail badly in this form; and his failures seem to occur

when he uses the supernatural to explain situations into which he has written himself without being able to conceive of a way out. Moreover, he sometimes abandons the most carefully built framework for a quick exit from a story, and he does so quite without artistic conscience.

Among the better stories is "The Ancient Sin"[30] in which Tarlyon and Trevor, while taking a ride in the country, are stopped by a distraught old woman. She leads them to a farmhouse in the woods where an old patriarch is beating his son: " 'Friends,' said the old man, and his was the voice of authority, 'you must leave me in peace to drive the sin out of this my son. His mother is a woman and will pardon everything in those she loves, but you are men and know the one sin that is unpardonable by all men!' " While he speaks, his son seizes a shovel and kills him.

As the two men go for the police, they wonder at what the sin might be: "You and I, Ralph, and our friends, have become so civilised that we don't know what the unpardonable sins are. We simply don't *know*, old man! . . . We are so civilised that we pardon too much—both in ourselves and other people; and we call that being broad-minded, but it's really being flabby. But that old man, I'm sure, was not 'broad-minded,' he was as little broad-minded as Jehovah, and there was one sin he simply would not pardon. And we, who are civilised people, do not even know what it was. . . ."

When they return to the scene of the crime with the constable, they find that the house, a burned-out shell, has been uninhabited for years; and only the silk handkerchief with which they had tied the boy remains to indicate the place. The sergeant tells them that a parricide had occurred there thirty years ago; the boy was pardoned, "being judged mad." The men depart, having learned a lesson, "for the face of the sergeant of police was the grown face of the lunatic boy," and "the one sin that the old man said was unpardonable by all men is blasphemy." The message of this story is that civilization and sophistication are accompanied by moral decay; carelessness in speech and action are dangerous in a world of forces we cannot understand.

In "The Gentleman from America"[31] a practical joke played by two Englishmen on an American has tragic results. Puce, the American, is promised money if he can stay the night in a

"haunted" house in Grosvenor Square. The events of the night—
a spectral form appears, pistol shots are fired to no effect—drive
the American mad, as the two practical jokers, who had for their
own amusement stage-managed the entire evening, discover to
their distress years later. An "in" joke for Arlen cognoscenti lies
in the fact that the ghost story Puce reads before going to bed
was written by Ivor Marlay of "Piracy". Winningly macabre,
though slight in content, "The Gentleman from America" is
Arlen's most frequently anthologized story.

In "The Ghoul of Golders Green,"[32] Arlen lavishes enormous
attention on an awful story idea. Ralph Wyndham Trevor and
Beau Maturin encounter some seemingly supernatural events
which turn out to be the efforts of a movie company trying to
shoot a picture at low cost. Arlen, who spends fifty pages effectively telling the story, quite astonishingly throws it away with
a silly twist of plot. At such times, Arlen needed an editor who
could have suggested tactfully that he put the story away until
a better ending occurred to him.

"The Revolting Doom of the Man Who Would Not Dance
with His Wife"[33] deals with a jealous husband's murder of his
wife, whose crime was that she loved to dance, although her
husband could not. The ghost of the lady has a last waltz with
her husband's secretary before departing. This story connects
to the larger framework of Arlen's work. In *The Green Hat*,
the narrator amuses the convalescing heroine with an idea for
a story about a man who would not dance with his wife; he says
he can't figure out why, but he will write the story when he does.

O. Henry was, as we have observed, a powerful influence on
Arlen, as he himself cheerfully admitted; and Arlen wrote several
stories with "twist" endings that emphasize the ironies in life.
In "Where the Pigeons Go to Die"[34] a young lady, ignoring the
impulses of her heart, is killed while unwillingly fulfilling a
promise made years before. In "Fay Richmond"[35] an "ineligible"
young man does not woo a girl he loves because she is engaged;
but subsequent events prove that both would have been happier
if he had behaved less "honorably." In "The Shameless Behavior
of a Lord,"[36] an ambitious mother tries to make a match between
her daughter and the fabulously wealthy Lord Paramour. When
Lord Paramour explains that, because of principle, he could

marry no one he had not seen naked, the mother invites him for a weekend and inveigles her daughter into a convenient outdoor bath. The next day she asks his opinion: " 'The only thing I'm not sure about,' whispered Lord Paramour, 'is whether I like her nose. Sorry, I'm sure.' "

VI "The Romance of Iris Poole"

More ambitious than any of the short stories considered thus far is "The Romance of Iris Poole,"[37] a psychological *novella* which traces the fatal competition of two brothers, Roger and Antony Poole. Four characters dominate the action. Iris Poole, the fiercely loyal wife of Roger, has "nothing of the *femme fatale* about her," but she has a "wonderful talent for obsessing men." Roger Poole, the elder brother and Iris's husband, is successful at business, politics, and love. Antony Poole, younger by a year, is a failure in all the spheres of his brother's success; and is wracked with destructive jealousy because of it. Ronnie, the observer-narrator, is a sympathetic friend who describes the destruction of the family. Ronnie later marries Iris.

The competition between the brothers causes the crisis when, after having been estranged for years, they are reunited by the well-meaning Iris. Antony, jealous of his brother in all ways, and especially of his marriage to Iris, contrives Roger's ruin and, unintentionally, his death, by involving him in a business swindle. When Antony leaves incriminating evidence where the police can find it, Roger, faced with jail as well as financial ruin, shoots himself. However, Arlen's primary interest lies not in the plot but in the delineation of the relationship between the brothers. Roger traces the roots of Antony's resentment to their childhood and specifically to the advent of a tutor and to the necessity for the brothers to settle down to work. Always the favored child because of his vivacity, Antony finds himself outmatched by his brother both in book learning and, later in school, in athletics. When Roger also succeeds in marrying Iris, who is loved by both brothers, Antony's desire for revenge commences. Some point is given to Roger's death by his analysis of Antony; for, as he sees it, their fate is inescapable: Antony's obsessive jealousy will never let him rest until he destroys

Roger. Roger, for his part, recognizes that his life is forever incomplete without his brother. Iris provides the occasion for the denouement, but the brothers' fate is sealed without her.

Arlen attempts in this story to diagnose the mysteries of success and love. Roger treats Iris badly in their marriage. As he comes to see, he was unhappy because he had won her as easily as he had everything else in life; and this easy conquest had made him value her less. As Antony involves Roger deeper in ruination through faulty investments and shady deals, Roger shows another side of himself—one which to Iris is much more valuable because it is accessible to love: "The vivid fact [was] that I was intensely glad at the failure of his luck! All those arrogances and dominations with which he had first charmed, then repelled, and always baffled one ... the whole of his easy mastery over life that had bred his 'confidence,' 'vitality'—I saw now that they were just the scum over his good-luck, a kind of verdigris that had made me grow to despise him, however unwillingly.... The man was everything, the luck worse than nothing." Antony kills more than he can possibly know, for the new Roger has finally realized Iris's value to him, and he is able to truly love her for the first time.

Arlen uses a shifting point of view adroitly in "The Romance of Iris Poole." Ronnie, the narrator, tells at some time after the action what he knows from his own interested but removed position. Iris, married at last to Ronnie, tells portions of the story as a key participant and describes the fluctuations of her own feelings; and, for great stretches, Iris quotes Roger to Ronnie, thereby providing at third hand the commentary of the one closest to the maelstrom. Antony, the heart of the mystery, is seen solely through the eyes of the other three.

In "The Smell in the Library,"[38] a sequel to "The Romance of Iris Poole," Antony returns to London and pays for his crimes. Wealthy again, he purchases his brother's house, restores the library to the precise state it was in when Roger shot himself, and places himself there in darkness, night after night, to re-create the situation of Roger's suicide. Antony Poole's nemesis is the mysterious woman he has married, Diavalen, a Creole; for she frightens him to death by reproducing the odor of the suicide bullet during his night vigil. George Tarlyon and Ralph Wyndham-Trevor are horrified witnesses to the scene that follows: "Diavalen was laughing—the dumb woman was laughing with all the glory of ivory teeth and scarlet lips.... We left the thing to its joke. We went out by the window, and did not remember our hats and sticks." We may quarrel with Arlen's turning a psychological tale into a witch story, but the sequel was praised by several reviewers of *These Charming People*.[39]

VII "The Prince of the Jews"

When asked in 1930 to contribute to an anthology entitled *My Best Story*,[40] Arlen chose "The Prince of the Jews,"[41] a story which had appeared in two significantly different versions in *May Fair* and in the July, 1925, issue of *Redbook*, in which it bears the title "The Knife Thrower." The Prince of the Jews is young Julian Raphael, a handsome, sensual, elusive criminal sought by Scotland Yard for counterfeiting, drug-smuggling, pandering, and murder. A Socialist as well, Raphael contrives to insult the upper-class protagonist, Charles Fasset-Smith, a naval officer. The quarrel between them is intensified by Raphael's mistress, Manana Cohen, who is attracted to Fasset-Smith and tries to shield him from harm despite Raphael's hatred and jealousy. When Fasset-Smith and his friend George Tarlyon, who are earnestly playing at being amateur detectives, track Raphael to his hideout, a dangerous confrontation occurs; and Raphael's knife narrowly misses Fasset-Smith. Following this encounter, Manana secretly goes to Fasset-Smith's home to warn him that her lover is determined to kill him. Raphael, who has followed her, hurls another knife at Fasset-Smith but kills Manana when she leaps into the way. The distraught Raphael disappears after vowing to kill his intended victim some day.

In the weeks that follow, the English admiral imagines several nightly encounters with Raphael outside his club. One evening, ducking from the imagined sound of a knife thrown at him, Fasset-Smith is struck by an automobile and immediately killed. His spirit arises from his dead body, however, to be greeted by the forms of Manana and of Raphael, who had died abroad while planning his revenge. United after death, the three fall into an amicable friendship; however, Raphael, because of his sins, has to accept the relationship that has developed between Fasset-Smith and Manana.

The cheap sentimentalism of the story's ending is regrettable, to say the least; and it is more so because of the vitality of the beginning. The style is engaging, however; and the characters are entertainingly, if not realistically, drawn. Fasset-Smith—a friend of Napier and Venice Harpenden of *The Green Hat*— is as attracted to the grace and charm of Julian Raphael as he is challenged by his arrogance; and Manana's beauty and concern for him touch Fasset-Smith romantically. Raphael lacks complexity, but his energetic single-mindedness makes him a vivid figure.

The title character of the *Redbook* story, "The Knife Thrower"— which seems clearly to be the earlier of the two versions—is similar in all respects to Julian Raphael, except that his name is Aram Valerian and he is an Armenian. As such, he is still an outsider, an exotic alien; but the shift in nationality transforms the story into yet another of Arlen's efforts to reconcile his "Eastern" temperament with that of the Western world. Such a psychological interpretation of the story does not improve its flawed ending, but it perhaps explains why Arlen thought the story his best.

VIII "Farewell, These Charming People"

"Farewell, These Charming People,"[42] a rambling, but often delicious satire, presents a Shavian Mephistopheles named Captain Charity who comments on human and divine nature at a dinner party to which Arlen has summoned his gallery of characters. In Arlen's incarnation, Satan is rather more Promethean than evil; he is dedicated to preventing the sacrifice of "the spirit of man to the savagery of mankind." Revolting against God's "ignorant and warlike complacency," he was defeated and sent to hell. Thwarted in his rebellion, he has spent his life directing "mankind to fulfill its most childish dreams and to sink into Nature's bosom, wherein only can be found true joy, true love, and perfect peace." As a result, he made the Greek and Roman civilizations flourish until God sent Paul "to revive the savagery in men." Since then, God has ruled the world.

Satan's diatribe is placed in a tale of rivalry between two

London hostesses—Lady Surplice of an old, established family; and Mrs. Amp, an upstart American. With the death of Mrs. Amp, who is eaten by circus lions, Lady Surplice seems to have won; but she is infuriated when Captain Charity tells her that Mrs. Amp gives dinner parties in hell that are attended by such worthies as Julius Caesar, Shakespeare, Pepys, and Balzac. Lady Surplice seems barred from entering into competition with Mrs. Amp, for she, as a virtuous woman, is destined for heaven. But Shelmerdene saves the day by telling Captain Charity that Lady Surplice is, in fact, a murderer: she had once bored a lover to death. Reluctantly, he bears her off to hell, where the competition is presumably renewed.

Arlen seems to have modeled his story upon the real-life competition between two rival hostesses, Mrs. Ronald Greville and Lady Maud Cunard. Mrs. Greville, well-established socially, had inherited breweries from her father and had entertained royalty; Maud Cunard, born an American, had owned very little and had had as her sole royal contact the Prince of Wales; but she had proved an aggressive and influential rival, as well as a patron of the arts. We may compare an account of Lady Cunard's famous and, to some, "devastating" introductions— "Here is Lady Diana Cooper, who is the most beautiful woman in the world, and here is Mr. Winston Churchill, who is the greatest orator since Bright, and here is Mr. George Moore, who is an immortal, and here is Madame Pavlova, who is another immortal, and here is the Duke of Westminster, who owns the whole of Westminster Square"[43]—with Arlen's description of Lady Surplice's technique:

This is Miss Pamela Star, who was left many millions by an Armenian. Armenians are rather difficult, my dear Captain Charity, but she is charming. And this is Shelmerdene, who has no surname because she has no surname, but who is becoming the heroine of all the ladies in all the suburbs because a misguided young man once put her into a book. Ah, and Fay! My dear Captain Charity, this is Lady Fay Paradise, the most beautiful woman in England. She never eats with her meals and never uses the same lover twice. Do you, darling? Whereas here is Lady Amelia Peep, who is as yet unmarried, but she writes poetry about birds and her father wants to be made a Duke. You will like her. She is appointed with every modern convenience.[44]

Lady Cunard once dragged the reluctant novelist across a room to announce, loudly, "This is Michael Arlen—the only Armenian who has not been massacred!"[45] Arlen seems to have devised a particularly entertaining revenge.

To understand Arlen's achievement as a writer of short stories we must first recognize that he was not an experimenter in new forms but the skillful exploiter of old ones. Of the movement away from personal narrative, in which the author's voice disappears—the movement of which Katherine Mansfield and James Joyce, following the lead of Chekhov, were leading exponents—Arlen had no part. He relied on his narrative voice, with its knowing intonations of sophistication, gentle mockery, and keen wit, to bind his readers; he used it to teach them to appreciate themselves and their manners and to laugh at their pretensions. The years have not diminished the charm of that voice.

Arlen closes *May Fair* with the claim that he has "told the last adventures of *These Charming People*." He seems to have meant it, too, despite the fact that he occasionally trotted out a member of his repertory company for appearance in some new tale. But he had caught the public ear not merely to charm it, but because he felt he had something to say. In any case, 1925— the year *May Fair* appeared—marks the end of this period in his creative life. In the years that followed, he wrote better but never with as much popular success.

CHAPTER 4

The Green Hat

I *Plot*

ADVERTISEMENTS appeared in 1924 that announced Michael Arlen's next book, a major work to be called "The Dark Angel." Reportedly, Arlen completed it, decided it was a failure, destroyed it, and then intensively wrote *The Green Hat* in two months. Subtitled *A Romance for a Few People*, the book was an immediate, sustained success. *The Green Hat* (1924) concerns a love relationship that was once thwarted by parental and social pressure, that endured eleven years of separation, and that was thwarted again by a noble act of self-sacrifice. Its heroine, Iris March, is condemned by public opinion as immoral, but the novel's last-minute revelation proves her to be the guardian of an ideal. She has surrendered herself to public disgrace in order to protect the reputation of another.

At the age of eighteen, Iris is separated from Napier Harpenden, the man she loves, by his snobbish and ambitious father. She marries a mutual friend, "Boy" Fenwick, a young man idolized by his generation; but a scandal ensues when Fenwick commits suicide on their wedding night. Iris explains to her friends that he died "for purity"—and she permits them to interpret her remark to her detriment. Her second husband, Hector Storm, dies in a military campaign in Ireland after having been driven to volunteer for service by hearing his wife murmur Napier's name in her sleep. The reader first meets her as Iris Storm, twice-widowed woman of many affairs, visiting her alcoholic twin brother.

Gerald March, the brother, is an idealistic, hypersensitive young man who resents his sister's immoral life. He has refused to see her for ten years because of Fenwick's suicide; but, because she plans to leave England shortly, she impulsively visits him after midnight. She asks the narrator, a stranger to her, for help when Gerald does not answer her knocking. When they enter the flat and find Gerald drunk and unconscious, they retire to the narrator's nearby rooms where their conversation ends with their going to bed. When Iris leaves in the morning, she and the narrator remain friends, although their physical intimacy is not resumed.

On another night, several paths cross. In a public restaurant Napier, who is to be married in three days, meets Iris briefly, after eleven years of voluntary separation. On hearing the news that Gerald March has been arrested that afternoon for allegedly "annoying" a woman in Hyde Park, the narrator—an active character throughout the story, though he is never named—and Iris drive to Gerald's apartment. Gerald is dead, a suicide; but the narrator hides the fact from Iris in order temporarily to spare her feelings. As she drives away she is hailed from a second car—Napier's—and she and Napier, brought together by chance, drive off. They briefly resume their love affair, but Napier's marriage takes place as scheduled.

Ten months later, the narrator discovers Iris in Paris, deathly ill after giving birth to a stillborn child. When Napier also arrives, his appearance encourages Iris to continue living. He has not, however, been told of her pregnancy; and he believes her illness to have been caused by food poisoning. Several months later, Napier and Iris meet again in London and resolve to elope. To divert Iris from the plan, Guy de Travest, an older friend of the Harpenden and March families, arranges a drive to the country for himself and three couples, including Napier and his wife Venice and the narrator and Iris. After a dangerous, careless ride they arrive after midnight at a country resort and go for a swim in the Thames. When Venice flounders in the darkness, Iris, though weakened by her recent illness, plunges into the water to save her. At the end of the evening, Iris's determination to take Napier and find the happiness denied her a decade earlier remains unshaken.

On the eve of their elopement, Iris accepts the challenge of Napier's father, Sir Maurice Harpenden, for a last-minute confrontation. When he roundly denounces her as a sinner and wrecker of homes and careers, she stoutly defends her right to the love which Sir Maurice had once before thwarted. Enraged, Harpenden accuses Iris of murdering Boy Fenwick, her first husband. At that moment Napier, who has arrived late on the scene, intervenes to reveal the secret truth that he himself has only recently discovered: Boy Fenwick had thrown himself out of the hotel window not, as everyone believed, in despair about Iris's confessions of immorality, but because of his own shame because he had syphillis.

Knowing that Fenwick was idealized by his generation and especially by her brother Gerald, Iris had protected his name from scandal, thereby preserving his reputation at the cost of her own, which was the true meaning of her assertion that Fenwick had died "for purity." But this revelation, which is a chastening shock to Sir Maurice, is deeply distressing to Iris, who tells Napier, "You have taken from me . . . the only gracious thing I ever did in my life" (344). She sends Napier back to his wife by telling him, falsely, that Venice is pregnant; then she drives into the night to crash her car into the tree under which, as children, she, Gerald, Napier, and Boy had played. In the aftermath, Napier and his wife—convinced that Iris's death was accidental—settle into an ordinary, respectable, but uninspired marriage: Venice sits at home while he travels and serves abroad.

II *Characters: Iris*

The major character, as well as the major critical problem, of the book is Iris. That she was in her day accepted by many readers as a realistic portrait is demonstrated by the book's great popularity and by the interest readers took in her morality and in her life-style. Generally, she dresses casually, as if for travel, in a short leather coat. Her hat, in the repeated descriptive formula, is "bright green, of a sort of felt, and bravely worn: being, no doubt, one of those that women who have many hats affect *pour le sport*" (11). Stylistically, the "shameless, shameful lady" with the "tiger-tawny hair" is adorned in highlights and shadows: "It is not good to have a pagan body and a Chislehurst [Puritan] mind, as I have. It is hell for the body and terror for the mind" (58); "There is a curse on us, the Marches. . . . The Marches are never let off anything" (44); "She made not one gesture of womanhood. . . . She must meet men on their own ground always, always, and she must keep herself on their ground without showing the effort she made" (328–29). These dramatic, admiring phrases made Iris come alive for many readers; they also, of course, became prime targets for satirists and parodists.

Iris is, in the eyes of polite society, *déclassée* and, to some, a nymphomaniac. Arlen explains her condition as being the result of strong sexual drives aggravated by the frustration of her ideal childhood love for Napier. As children, Gerald and Iris March had played with Napier Harpenden and Boy Fenwick. Gerald idolized Boy, while Napier and Iris fell in love. And although Sir Maurice separated the young pair at eighteen because he considered the Marches "rotten" stock, the love endured, especially in Iris. At their separation Iris had told Napier, "I think I have a body that burns for love. Napier, I shall burn it with love, but I will never say 'I love you' to any man but you, because it will never be true." Recalling those words later in life, she adds, "What I said at eighteen is true at thirty. . . . I have given myself, in disdain, in desire, with disgust, with delight, but I have kept to that silly, childish boast of mine" (314). But because all her lovers are inadequate substitutes for Napier, sex has been a torment to Iris, as she explains to the narrator: "I am not what you think. I am not of the women of your life. I am not the proud adventuress who touches men for pleasure, the silly lady who misbehaves for fun. I am the meanest of all, she who destroys her body because she must, she who hates the thing she is, she who loathes the thing she does. . . . To be born a chaste woman . . . is good. I am in favor of chastity" (58). In other words, Iris is not a crusader for sexual freedom but a Puritan at heart who is driven to promiscuity by her physical needs, despite her secret idealism.

A similar idealism exists in her attitude towards Napier's career and towards the values held dear by Sir Maurice—the values that led to the frustration of her love. During her final interview with Napier's father she explains her antagonism:

I despise your England. . . . You would have Napier toil for a worm's reward, you are sorry I have broken Napier's career in the Foreign Office. Maurice, I am glad. To you, it seems a worthy thing for a good man to make a success in the nasty arena of national strifes and international jealousies. To me, a world which thinks of itself in terms of puny, squalid, bickering little nations and not one glorious field for the crusade of mankind is a world in which to succeed is the highest indignity that can befall a good man, it is a world in which good men are shut up like gods in a lavatory. (330–31)

Thus Iris voices Arlen's suspicion of nationalism, urging its replacement by higher loyalties.

Given the sensational incidents and the social background of the novel, Arlen could have taken a variety of approaches to his material. He chose—or had his narrator choose—to accept, admire, and even idolize Iris:

I couldn't help thinking of her as of some one who had strayed into our world from a strange land unknown to us, a land where lived a race of men and women who were calmly awaiting their inheritance of our world when we should have annihilated one another in our endless squabbles about honour, morality, nationality. . . . [Iris's face] knew not truth nor lying, not honour nor dishonour, not loyalty nor treachery, not good not evil: it was profoundly itself, a mask of the morning of this world when men needed not to confuse their minds with laws with which to confuse their neighbours, a mask of the evening of this world when men shall have at last made passions their servants and can enter their full inheritance. (268–69)

This awe is not supported by the Iris of this novel, even after the revelation of her great self-sacrifice. But, giddy and untenable as the attitude towards Iris and towards the "new world" may be, and unworthy as Iris is of serious consideration as a character, she is a bold attempt at the grand manner, a figure who asserts, in matters unrelated to sexuality at least, a single standard for men and women, and who defends the primacy of human relationships over deadening traditions. She may not seem to us, today, an adequate vehicle for such ideals, but obviously she provided for many readers a powerful symbol of what the "new" woman might be.

Iris engaged the imaginations of so many because her mystique revealed the existence of and helped shape a new community of sensibilities, one linked to the "'new sophistication'" lamented by the older generation, to the shedding of Victorianism, and to postwar disillusionment (most notably, perhaps, in the exposing of the "ideal" young man, Boy Fenwick). But, at the same time, the book hedged its bets: it balanced its daring "newness" with bows to the old values; therefore, it sounded precisely the right note and resonated richly—for Arlen, very richly—in the popular imagination.

There is, however, no rescuing Iris as a character in whom a reader can fully believe. She is a fabricated composite, "a very young man's dream of a woman—experience plus innocence, a prostitute with the soul of a virgin," as one hostile, contemporary commentator asserted.[1] In real terms, Iris is neurotic, not saintly; her motives are unbelievable and her sacrifices gratuitous, especially the final one. Why, if she rejected Sir Maurice's values so strongly that she could run away with Napier and ruin his future, should the revelation of Boy Fenwick's imperfections cause her to kill herself—especially with Gerald dead, for whom the sainted memory of Fenwick did little good while he had lived? Asking such questions causes the fabric of the novel to disintegrate, as many critics have already suggested.

One explanation of Arlen's lapses may be that he was too enthralled by his source of inspiration, the brilliant, unconventional Nancy Cunard. Daphne Fielding, in her book about Emerald and Nancy Cunard, states flatly that Arlen loved Nancy Cunard "very deeply" during this period.[2] Although the fact that Nancy Cunard provided the basis for the portrait of Iris was clear to many, her own reaction was quite amiable: "The Baron," as she called Arlen, "made a lot of money with *The Green Hat*—and for such nonsense too—but no need to begrudge him that."[3]

III *Napier and Venice*

Arlen's portrayal of the other characters also suffers under scrutiny. Napier is incredibly obtuse. Too weak to stand up to his father at eighteen, he is too dense at twenty-nine to understand what has happened to Iris. He has an affair with her on the eve of his wedding and then drops her and proceeds with his marriage; after a year, he changes his mind and abandons the marriage—as the narrator disgustedly states, "first to stain what he thinks his 'honour' by taking a mistress, and then to retrieve his idiotic 'honour' by hurting his mistress" (232). But, despite this harsh judgment, the narrator also admires Napier as "a strange, secret, saintly youth, a favourite of the gods who never once relied on the favouritism of the gods or men" (190). Napier's vacuity is never judged in a way that matches the reader's second thoughts.

As for Venice, she is a very strange girl indeed. Iris shrewdly comments that her near-drowning was done "on purpose ... so I should like her" (299)—a fittingly devious motive under those circumstances. But, in the end, Venice cheers Iris for her effort to rescue Napier—from her, of course, but mainly from respectability and Sir Maurice: "I'm enchanted too ... by the love of Napier and Iris. I'd stuff all our marriage laws down a drainpipe rather than keep them apart for another minute" (341). Finally, Venice too is impossible; she is a too convenient means of maintaining the reader's uncomplicated sympathy for the fleeing lovers and for focusing hostility on Sir Maurice Harpenden, the villain.

IV *The Narrator*

The major characters—Iris especially—were endlessly discussed and analyzed by commentators and reviewers. One factor that didn't receive the attention it deserved, but which accounts heavily for the book's success, is the characterization of the narrator, a full and interesting figure, who is truer to life than anyone else in the novel. Well-meaning, fumbling, awed by Iris and half in love with her, he filters the events of the story through his sympathetic but never quite adequate understanding of the protagonists. He is, on the night of Iris's first arrival, a distressed and unhappy person. He has returned from a party he did not enjoy; his flat is depressing and, in the confusion of moving, a mess: "There lay the disorder of my life, the jumble, the lack of purpose, the silence, and the defeat of my life" (29). When Iris arrives in her marvelous Hispano-Suiza automobile, her glamor overwhelms him: "Dingy—that is what I felt before this quiet, thoughtful woman" (25).

The narrator's vision of Iris as of another and superior order of beings is the reason, he explains, that he "felt so profoundly incapable with her. . . . I am a man of my time. For that is a limitation a man can't get beyond—to be of his time, completely. He may be successful, a man like that—indeed, should he not blow his brains out if he is not?—but he who is of his time may never rise above himself. . . . And so I had with this woman that profound sense of incapacity, of defeat, which any limited man must feel with a woman whose limitations he cannot know" (31). The description and conception of the lady may be naïve and incomplete, but the responses of the limited narrator are convincingly revealed.

As they talk through the night hours and it becomes apparent that Iris is in no mood to leave, the narrator woos her, not very aggressively or purposefully, but effectively. When he finds her on his bed, however, he is "seized by a catholic anger": "Through all the disenchantments of youth, despite the contagious impurities of life, in defiance of the crimes against love that we call love, I had kept romance for my ghostly companion. Romance was more than a silly lithe goddess coming down from a marble column. . . . To romance, which was the ultimate vision of commonsense, sex, as sex, was the most colossal bore that had ever distracted man from his heritage. And she would palm a facet of this colossal bore off on me!" (52). Setting aside the excess of the protest, the point is that the narrator—a commonplace man, who is doomed, as he sees it, to success in a commonplace world—keeps a dream and an ideal to himself that Iris might fulfill but which, sex-driven as she is, her mere physical offering cannot supply.

Despite these feelings, the narrator earns Iris's everlasting affection by making one gratuitous but highly effective gesture. "God bless you, dear," Iris says when leaving; and, when the narrator responds, "He has, with Iris Storm," she is deeply touched: "She went very white. 'That shall be written down,' she whispered, 'as the prayer of the only man who ever shamed a woman of her shame'" (59). Later in the book she explains why she considers him her only friend: "Because once upon a time you shamed me of my shame. Because you did not hold me cheap. Because romance dies hard in you" (308). We see

Arlen straining hard with this contrivance—he needs a motive to tie the narrator into a confidential relationship with his heroine —but the idea that Iris had never before had a lover who treated her respectfully, or even kindly, seems very unlikely.

As an active participant in the plot, the narrator intervenes at two crucial points: once, when he fails to tell Iris of her brother's suicide, and thereby sends her into the night for the accidental meeting with Napier; again, when he misinforms Napier of the nature of Iris's confinement, calling it ptomaine poisoning rather than the pregnancy-related illness it is. But though his actions have a great effect on the lives of Napier and Iris, he comfortably comments: "To me, the way I see it, it looks as though certain things were decreed to happen and that, therefore, they did happen: they had it in their blood, these people, that certain things should happen to them, and I could no more contrive these things than they could evade them" (60). For the narrator, in view of the disasters that follow, determinism is obviously a comforting philosophic stance; he is not responsible but is merely an unwitting agent of fate.

Throughout the novel, the narrator tries to reconcile his pedestrian moral tendencies and his romantic impulses. On the one hand, he really disapproves of Iris's hasty affair with Napier on the eve of his marriage: "Iris was the foe. Why shouldn't she die? You can't do things like that, and not die. Stealing like a little thief into the garden of Venice, and stealing away like a little thief . . . to bear Napier's child, unknown to Napier" (197). The love of Napier and Iris is "damnable madness," he concludes, and it should be denied because of Venice. On the other hand, the narrator condemns Napier for his very adherence to the principles which link him to Venice: "Never were two men so different as Napier and me. I, I would have broken my troth, that is what I would have done, and I would have broken away from any other thing that stood in the way of my passion. I would have fled father, friends, career, honour, everything, at the call of the enchanted voice, whispering of better dreams" (232–33). The narrator speaks as a man free of Napier's class and family duties, as one whose romantic side sees that men of Napier's sort "often only find themselves when they have lost themselves" (233).

The narrator, then, though a man of fluid views, is nonetheless an arbiter of the novel's values whose sympathetic concern makes him a valuable commentator. The novel moves as it does because he is always there to glamorize Iris by his attitude—a mixture of criticism, awe, and devotion. Capable of ironic detachment from everything else, he is enthralled by the mystery of Iris's affections. This tension is both the novel's strength—because the psychology of the individual trapped between value structures is valid—and its weakness—because the narrator doesn't really understand life's Iris Marches or the points at which the character fades into narrative contrivance. The narrator's charm is Arlen's; and so are his ultimate limitations as a witness.

V   Reviews

The Green Hat was greatly admired by the reviewer for the *New York Times*, who called it "a provocative novel, written with skill and insight, a sensitive story and a character portrait." Iris is a "brilliant portrait of a passionate, intelligent, suffering woman, which Arlen realizes with a consummate and probing pity." The reviewer also praised Arlen's imagery, his "sonorous prose," his "keen levity," his "grace and charm," his "deft phrasing," and his "searching and profound observations." The reviewer concluded that *"The Green Hat* is almost perfect technique. . . . It rises to a gradual dramatic close that is inevitable. A finely wrought, sound piece of work, for the ending is an achievement that any modern novelist might well be proud of, a challenge to perfect craft."[4] Little wonder that some people thought Arlen loomed as a major literary figure, one in the category of James and Conrad.

Most reviewers, however, evinced more grudging admiration. To Stark Young, the novel was "mostly tosh but done often with brilliance, subtle insinuation, and smart craft."[5] Writing in the *Saturday Review of Literature*, Clarence Bray Hammond asked, "Why does Michael Arlen load down his witty, shining stuff with a plot? . . . Michael Arlen is the kind of person who gets away with murder. He tells you confidently things that wouldn't take in a goose." The book's theme, he suggests, is "that a bad person may really be very good—especially if her hair and other things about her are beautiful."[6] The reviewer in the *Times Literary Supplement* asserted that "it has never been possible to question this writer's cleverness, but it has sometimes been impossible not to doubt...his artistic sincerity." Uncertain whether Arlen's "pleasant" cynicism or his romantic sentiment is more basic to him, the reviewer says of Iris that "it is with a sense of having been cheated that we witness her final white-washing in the last chapter, with its perfunctory inevitable self-sacrifice."[7]

In *The Modern Novel* (1926), Elizabeth A. Drew, though calling the book opportunistic in its treatment of characters and finding Iris's noble lie "entirely ridiculous," suggests a serious and useful purpose behind the novel: "With all this semi-smart, tormented writing and all the emotional tomfoolery, there is the really bold new acceptance of the sins of the flesh as venial and inessential as compared with the quality of the spirit. In a pitifully milk-and-barley-water, backboneless way, the writer is trying to say the same thing as the author of *Tom Jones* and, by making his hero a heroine, to emphasize...the twentieth century doctrine of the single standard of sexual morality."[8] Clearly the book had many facets: if one reviewer did not care for the style, the sentiment was present; if another despised the sentiment, there was the cynicism; and behind the cynicism it was possible to discern a message.

Looming large among those who detested the novel was the sardonic George Jean Nathan, H. L. Mencken's colleague at *The Smart Set*, who seemed never to tire in his ceaseless public flogging of *The Green Hat*. Summarizing his criticism of the work in an article in *American Mercury*, Nathan suggests that Arlen makes his greatest appeal to the semieducated: "Wherever one finds persons open-mouthed before The Second Hungarian Rhapsody, the 'William Tell Overture' and the performances of Ukelele Ike...one finds coincidently impassioned devotees of the Arlen art." To Nathan, Arlen's stories are "rented dress suit literature," his prose is that of "the fashionable world of Mr. Cecil B. De Mille," and his average heroine is "a couturier's idea of a romantic lady." Nathan credits Arlen only for his ability to tell a story and for "an occasionally nice wit. And so it is that he goes down the reading public's gullet like Epsom salts."[9]

Harsher than Nathan's is Professor William York Tindall's judgment: "The manner of *The Green Hat* is warm, pink, and confidential. As Mayfair dotes on cocktails, he invokes the mews, and all the nymphomaniacs and drunks assume for him a kind of glamor. Arlen saw society, but, misunderstanding its meaning, made the desperate meretricious, the horrid shoddy."[10]

Of satires of the novel there were many. In *This Charming Green Hat-Fair*, Barry Pain populated Mayfair with such characters as Halfa Gale (Iris March's married name was Storm) and Guy de Travesty. As "Halfa" sees things, and as some readers thought Arlen saw them, "society today is founded on the solid rock of promiscuity and polygamy, and the avoidance of all responsibilities—particularly the parental. Who was the stuffy old Victorian who bleated about conduct? Why, it doesn't matter what you do, if your heart be only true."[11] *Arabella* by "Eric Frisch" (a pseudonym) is "a story about a young man suffering from an attack of sophistication and an overdose of Michael Arlen's fantasies, indulged in just before sleeping."[12] Corey Ford, writing a series of parodies in various styles for Doran's *The Bookman* of January, 1926, took Sherlock Holmes and his assistants, The Rover Boys, to Mayfair to solve the Boy Fenwick case. "You are not a bad woman, Iris March," concludes Sherlock Holmes; "you are just bad grammar."[13] *Life* published the perhaps inevitable cartoon in which the woman asserts, "I have a pagan body but a puritan mind"; and the man asks hopefully, "Are you ever absent-minded?"[14]

Towards his own work Arlen displayed a becoming capacity for detachment. Informed that Charles Chaplin had called the romance of Iris and Napier "the greatest love story since *Romeo and Juliet*," he replied, "Naturally they continued deeply in love. They hadn't seen one another for twelve years."[15] In *The Green Hat* itself, we find the description of a commercially successful novelist who "had observed that the whole purpose of a 'best-seller' is to justify a reasonable amount of adultery in the eyes of suburban matrons," and Arlen courts disaster by observing that "in no current English novel was there ever a mention of any woman having a lover because she wanted a lover: she always took a lover because something had upset her, as in real life she might take an aspirin" (124). If a reader chose to laugh at *The Green Hat* instead of taking it seriously, he found Arlen an agreeable coconspirator.

In the final analysis, *The Green Hat* remains a period piece, a best-seller whose force as literature does not extend beyond its time. Arlen took on the task of accounting for a complex human being, a woman who compelled strong opposition and strong loyalty among those who knew her, and who appeared representative of new currents and aspirations among women. But Arlen did not confront his creation in her full complexity; he settled instead for the familiar contrivances offered by popular literary tradition.[16] The style, too, for all its Jamesian trappings—its pose of investigation and analysis—serves often as an artifice to disguise a simplistic vision.

Nonetheless, from the vantage point of the present, we should not underestimate the power of Arlen's story to affect the romantic side of its readers' imaginations. Svetlana Alliluyeva, daughter of Joseph Stalin, writes of her father's reaction to her mother's suicide: "It was only in his last years, not long before he died, that he suddenly started talking to me about it, nearly driving me out of my mind. I saw that he was desperately looking for the reason—looking and not finding it. Suddenly he would start denouncing the 'vile book' which my mother had read not long before she died. It was *The Green Hat* by Michael Arlen."[17]

CHAPTER 5

Playwright and Celebrity

I Dear Father, *or* These Charming People

B Y the end of 1924 Michael Arlen had published five books, attracted a good deal of public attention, and gained the respect of at least a portion of the literary world. He turned, then, for a time, to writing for the stage and the movies, and his career carried him, on a flood of publicity, from London to New York and Hollywood. Arlen had first tried his hand at playwriting, in an unserious way, for Orage in the pages of *The New Age*. However, his first work to be produced was a comedy called *Dear Father* which, starring Herbert Marshall and Isabel Jeans, opened on November 30, 1924, at the New Scala Theatre in London.

The text is apparently not extant, but from the reviews it appears that the plot concerns a young woman's efforts to rid herself of a boring husband. Her problems begin when the man she has chosen to be the corespondent is discovered to be the son of her father's butler, and the comedy develops from the vehement objections of the butler to the immorality of his employer's family. Arlen apparently tried unsuccessfully to impose a serious ending on the play, for the reviewer in the London *Times* objected that while *Dear Father* had worked well as a vehicle for Arlen's epigrams, the play could not sustain the weight of a heavier theme. The reviewer concluded that, despite the laughs the play engendered, its atmosphere was like "a warmed scent spray flourished by a rather indecisive barber."[1]

The next year, in the aftermath of the success of the play version of *The Green Hat*, Arlen transferred *Dear Father* to Broadway, changing its name to *These Charming People*. Herbert Marshall remained in the cast, but he was replaced in the leading role by the English comic actor Cyril Maude, who announced his appearance in the play as his farewell to the American stage. The New York production, which opened on October 6, 1925, and received fair reviews, seems to have been played more broadly than the London version, for the cast at one point in the action was released from the script and given free scope to posture, clown, and declaim. The *New York Times* reviewer felt that the piece had little intrinsic merit, but he remarked that Cyril Maude made good physical comedy of it anyway, "apart from the play."[2] In 1931 Cyril Maude starred in a film version of the play, again titled *Dear Father*, which was produced for Paramount British by Walter Morosco and directed by Louis Mercanton.

II The Green Hat *on Stage*

To write accurately of *The Green Hat* as a stage piece, we must treat the play as an event—an historical, cultural phenomenon—for such it was to its author, its audiences, and to the players who brought it to the stage. The play made stars of Katherine Cornell and Tallulah Bankhead, and it provided Greta Garbo, who played in the silent film version, with an excellent vehicle.[3] The contract for the New York production, which was to be the world premiere, was given to producer A. H. Woods, a Broadway veteran of many years in legitimate drama, vaudeville, melodrama, and bedroom farce. Woods, it was said, had declined to read the novel because it was too long; but on the basis of a plot summary, he set to work putting the cast together in 1924. Woods's first choice for the role of Iris was Jeanne Eagels, who had made a hit the year before as Sadie Thompson in William Somerset Maugham's *Rain*; but Woods finally took the script to Katherine Cornell, then a rising and respected young actress appearing in G. B. Shaw's *Candida*. She and her husband, Guthrie McClintick, had read the novel; and although McClintick had thought it "claptrap," Miss Cornell became interested in the possibilities of Iris as a stage character. When the offer came from Woods, McClintick, who was also Miss Cornell's director, opposed her accepting the role; but she prevailed, and early in 1925 she began rehearsals while still playing in *Candida*.[4]

Though Arlen was anxious to visit the United States to lend

advice to Woods and McClintick and to help stimulate publicity, the prospect of his arrival filled his American publisher, George Doran, with trepidation. When Doran had met Arlen in the summer of 1923 in London, he had noted the aura of success about the young author; and so, when Arlen's first American publisher had rejected *"Piracy"*, Doran had taken a shrewd risk, published it, and taken an option on Arlen's next three books. The gamble paid off handsomely: *These Charming People*, published in 1924, sold a hundred thousand copies in the United States, nearly a record for a book of short stories; and the American sales of *The Green Hat* were two hundred fifty thousand. But now, Doran feared, he might be courting disaster if Arlen, "as an unknown... a sensation and a hit," proved unsuccessful in his public appearances. As Doran later recalled, "Stupid wonderings and questions of mine! Michael came, he saw and was seen; he made conquests where conquering mattered."[5] Arlen assumed the mantle of a celebrity with the ease and grace of a man who had prepared a lifetime for it—as, in fact, he had.

After his arrival on March 10, 1925, Arlen was welcomed to New York by a series of dinners attended mainly by theater and literary people. He was expected to be witty, and he was. His dress was much discussed, especially his famous vests, which were the talk of the hotel staff. An interviewer has described him in these terms:

Mr. Arlen is slightly under average height, slim waisted, well knit, youthful in appearance. His hair is black and curly and he brushes it straight back. He has a ruddy skin and wears a toothbrush moustache that is sandy in color. He wears suits tailored with reinforced shoulders, pinched in at the waist, a trifle exaggerated in the current English mode. A colored silk handkerchief dangles from the outside breast pocket of his coat. He wears, during the day, colored shirts with collars of the like material, caught in tightly beneath the knot of his fancy tie, with a gold clasp. He talks easily and well; he has a sense of assurance and keenness.[6]

The same interviewer witnessed a luncheon with the Algonquin wits, that group of reigning American literati dubbed the "Vicious Circle," at which Arlen was mercilessly ragged—indeed, he was subjected to "the most trying ordeal I ever saw a guest of honor have to submit to." But, in the end, Arlen won all of them with his own wit and good humor.

Arlen had been greeted at the pier in New York by a delegation of Armenians. Uncharacteristically, he accepted an invitation to speak before the Armenian Educational Foundation, a group trying to preserve national identity and culture. His performance, while witty itself, showed the gap that had grown between him and them. He twitted them for their law-abiding qualities (in Prohibition time) by observing that "You have given me my first glass of water since landing in America." He chatted about whether male readers preferred short stories or novels. He told his audience not to be afraid of being lonely: "Loneliness in a big city gives one a sense of adventure"—showing that he had evidently forgotten his remarks in *The London Venture* about the "fools" and "knaves" who praise solitude. Commended for "admitting" his Armenian blood, he disapproved: "One doesn't admit to these things. I don't 'admit' I'm an Armenian. I merely 'say' I am one. I don't care what nationality a man is. He either does his job well or he doesn't. All the troubles in the world come from this driving at nationalities—jealousy, ill-will, warfare. Forget about it." Despite the fact that he told the members that their Armenian organization was futile, the crowd cheered him and shook his hand until it ached. He left early, saying that he had to attend a few other parties—presumably where people took Prohibition less seriously and appreciated a "sense of adventure."[7]

Arlen was quotable in himself and the cause of good quotations from others. "Why Mr. Arlen, you look almost like a woman," said Edna Ferber at a party he attended carrying, for some reason, a shepherd's crook. "So do you, Miss Ferber," he replied —which caused her to remember him unkindly in her autobiography.[8] Rebecca West called him "every other inch a gentleman," a line he liked so much he used it often himself.[9] Irwin Cobb professed to admire him for being "the only Armenian I have met who has not tried to sell me a rug."[10] Someone else suggested he was really Turkish propaganda sent to the United States to justify the Armenian massacres.[11] When asked by *Vanity Fair* to supply his own epitaph, he wrote: "Here lies

Michael Arlen—as usual."[12] He was, from all evidence, having a marvelous time.

Katherine Cornell, wearing a flowing silver gown and brandishing a huge sword, cut the cake at Arlen's welcoming party. Woods retained his doubts of her potential performance in the play, but Arlen saw her in *Candida* and approved the choice. After that, however, Arlen took no part in the production. Busy with his social life, he would rush to rehearsals, tell the cast they were doing splendidly, and rush off again; he wisely left the work to the sensible director and actors, who included, besides Miss Cornell, Leslie Howard (as Napier) and Ann Harding, who was replaced as Venice by Margalo Gilmore for the New York premiere. McClintick cut twenty minutes from the script, added suitable Arlenisms from other books, and generally tried to bind the play together.[13]

The play version spanned a decade in four acts.[14] In Act I, in which the action occurs the day after Boy's suicide, Iris tells her noble lie, despite the condemnation of her twin brother Gerald ("All we Marches are rotten, just rotten, and Iris is the worst of us") and Napier ("You've made my love as dirty as all Sodom and Gomorrah"); only the doctor who examined the body knows the truth, but Iris silences him with "Let's all do *one decent* thing in life!" In Act II, which takes place ten years later, Iris visits Napier, who is soon to marry Venice; and he discovers that the separation from Iris has not dampened his love for her. "When I look at you," he tells her, "it is as though this world, this England, the laws and the land of England, fade and pass from me like phantoms. They can't be phantoms, Iris." Passion overcomes them both, and the scene ends with this steamy exchange:

Iris (*whispering, crying*)—I am weak, weak!
Napier (*feverishly*)—What is it, Iris? What do you want?
Iris—What do I want! You, darling. (*She takes his head in her hands, drawing him to her. As they kiss, she reaches for the light switch and presses it.*)

This bit of staging became controversial. Miss Cornell recalls that the censor in Philadelphia was disturbed that the woman turned out the lights, but she insisted that it be played that way, for "To let the man do it put me in a much worse position." Miss Cornell also experimented with emphasis: to Napier's question, "What do you want?" she would normally answer, "*You*, baby"; for more sophisticated audiences, however, it was "You *baby*."[15] By scene two, Napier is willing to sacrifice his future for Iris; but she releases him: "Napier, you are bound to Venice by the strongest bond that can hold a decent man—her love for you."

Act III, which takes place nine months later, is set in the convent nursing home where Iris's baby has been stillborn. The ubiquitous Dr. Masters, who was in attendance in Act I in Deauville, is there, as are Napier and Venice. Miss Cornell, whose makeup for the scene (as she appears in photographs of the production) make her resemble the somnambulist in *The Cabinet of Dr. Caligari*, at one point takes Venice's hand and says, "I know who you are—You're Napier's pretty wife—you're pretty Venice. I saw a photograph of you once—and I said: 'She has such clean eyes. They frighten me.' But they don't frighten me any more. I'm too ill to be frightened of anything now." Critics were harsh about Act III. Alexander Woollcott said it reminded him of the sidewalk café of the Café de la Paix in Paris—that he was sure, if he stayed there long enough, he'd eventually meet everyone he ever knew.[16]

In Act IV, Iris faces Napier's father, Sir Maurice Harpenden, who denounces her for wanting to run away with his son: "Damn it, girl. This is evil. There aren't any words to describe what we think of a woman who comes between a man and his wife. . . . This strikes at the root of our life." Iris responds, "You want Napier to be a success. I want him to be a failure. The kind of success you respect is like a murky sponge wiping out the lines of a man's character." The remainder of the play resembles the novel: Napier reveals Iris's noble lie; Iris sends him back to Venice and then drives away to her suicide.

As may be seen from the excerpts quoted, Arlen's dramatic prose tended to grow overheated, presenting something of a challenge to the actors and actresses entrusted with bringing the characters to life. Furthermore, Katherine Cornell was taking something of a chance in playing Iris because she really wasn't

physically right for the part and because the character of Iris
in the novel, embedded in and embellished by Arlen's style,
might fail as a stage figure. However, by tactful shifts and
additions and mainly by adroit readings of the text, the cast
made the play successful. Katherine Cornell's concept of the
heroine helped: "I made Iris unobvious. Everything you would
expect her to do—smoke, drink, be seductive—I never did. I
made her a very quiet person. She taught me a lot about acting—
how to use a bad line—how to lick one. Such a line as, 'Boy died,
he died for purity.' You could lick it by smiling it—as if you were
saying, 'That's the worse nonsense I can think of. A catch phrase
that I know is bunky and you know is bunky and you know that
I know and I know that you know.'" The last scene, in which
Iris is condemned by the elder Harpenden, Miss Cornell staged
very subtly: throughout the tirade, she stood quite still, behind
a table, unconcernedly playing solitaire. Only when Napier burst
in and exposed her generous deception, thereby cheating Iris
of what she called "the only gracious thing I ever did," did Miss
Cornell drop her cards. The effect of the understated action,
Miss Cornell records, was electric.[17]

But, even while inventing all these clever ways of surmounting
the difficulties of the play, Miss Cornell was apprehensive during
rehearsals and out-of-town trials. Producer Woods brought Jeanne
Eagels to the opening in Detroit; but, if she had harbored any
hopes of getting the role, they must have been dashed when the
premiere went very well for Miss Cornell. Even McClintick
began to see the role's possibilities because of his wife's handling
of it. Out-of-town reviews were good—always for the acting;
sometimes for the play as well. Alexander Woollcott, who later
made considerable fun of the play, had good first impressions:
he reported from out of state to his New York readers that *The
Green Hat* was "a most absorbing play, distinguished by several
moments of still and steadfast beauty."[18]

As the play made its way through the Midwest, and reports
came in, public interest in it began to grow. Arlen's picture
appeared in department-store windows in displays of—what else?
—green felt hats, which were to be bravely worn, *pour le sport*,
by virgins and matrons hopeful of fashionable infamy.[19] By the
New York opening, publicity and public curiosity had reached

a high pitch. One spectator commented that "nothing quite like the opening of *The Green Hat* has been seen in New York since the Civil War draft riots. Men, women, and children struggled for tickets until prices in excess of one hundred dollars were offered for a single seat."[20]

New York critics were lukewarm about the play—several found it false and unconvincing—but Katherine Cornell's reviews were uniformly excellent. Dismissing the play as "flapdoodle" and "imitation Pineroticism," George Jean Nathan praised Miss Cornell as "head and shoulders above all the other young women of the American theatre." Robert Benchley called her "magnificent." Writing in the *Chicago Herald-Examiner*, Ashton Stevens, thinking of her admirable work in *Candida*, said he had been a bit dubious of her ability to change gears; but he had found her performance in *The Green Hat* "subtle; it was a little sinister; even, I fancied, a little pathological."[21] The performance made Katherine Cornell a star; she saw her name in lights for the first time while playing Iris March. She acted in the role from the first performance in Detroit on March 29, 1925, through its New York opening on September 15, where it ran twenty-nine weeks; and then she went on a tour with the play, all the way to Kansas City, during the summer of 1927.

Although things were going well for Miss Cornell, her leading man, Leslie Howard, was having great difficulty in keeping a straight face during performances. An out-of-town reviewer had suggested that the script be turned over to the Marx Brothers, who were then appearing in *The Coconuts*. Robert Benchley, in his review of Arlen's play, suggested a special matinee in which the actors could broaden their performances just an eighth of an inch and produce one of the great burlesques on Broadway. For Leslie Howard, one eighth of an inch seemed too generous by far; he thought the play burlesqued itself. His part as Napier was very difficult, for his lines were often grotesque when spoken, and they could not be handled ironically, as Miss Cornell's could. She gave him great credit for his handling of the part, as did some critics; but to one reviewer he played the role "like a young undertaker made somewhat uncomfortable by a sense of humor that he once possessed." Another suggested that he "might at least imitate something occasionally besides the Leaning

Tower of Pisa or whatever he thinks he is when he teeters
around all out of plumb."

Howard himself was quite ready to join the chorus of de-
tractors. Within a week of opening night, he was telling a
New York Herald Tribune reporter that "It's the hardest part
I ever had to play because I know that under the given circumstances nobody in the world would say the things I have to say
in the show." With Miss Cornell, the case was different, he said,
because "she is a colorful actress with a vivid personality that
rather shines in this sort of thing, while I am a drab sort of person
who can fit in only when the play is an exact picture of life."
Despite these feelings, the play was a success; and, despite
Howard's feelings, he tried to create a creditable part. His
daughter wrote of his experience:

No matter how it embarrassed him every night and twice on Wednes-
days and Saturdays, he held Katherine Cornell in his arms and told
her that she was "a woman with magic eyes and a soft, white body
that beats at my mind like a whip" and the public loved it. His
popularity increased every day. The women who sat beyond the
footlights, half faint with pleasure, imagined themselves clasped by
this glorious expounder of purple prose and heard him tell them:
"You are my dark angel and my tower of delight in the twilight of
the world."[22]

In Miss Cornell's recollections, one memorable evening towards
the end of the run—when the stage furniture had worn considerably—stands out:

At the end of the play you may remember that Iris kills herself
by driving her car against a tree. When Napier hears about this, he
cries, "It must have been an accident," and sinks into a chair. On
this particular night that old chair crumpled under his weight and
he was sprawled upon the floor. The actors were unable to restrain
their hysterical mirth and the audience followed suit. They quickly
got hold of themselves, however, and the house quieted down to hear
Venice deliver her next line which, unfortunately, read, "It wasn't
an accident." The final speech remained unspoken—the curtain
descended in a gale of laughter.[23]

But, by the time of this incident, Leslie Howard, who would have laughed hardest of all, had unfortunately left the cast.

The evening after the successful New York premiere of *The Green Hat* another Londoner scored a hit, one for which Michael Arlen was also partly responsible. Noel Coward, while staging his sensational play *The Vortex* in London the year before, had run short of funds. He had timidly approached Arlen, whom he had known for some years, and had been overwhelmed when his friend, flush with his new success as a writer of fiction, had written the required check without a second thought or even an interruption of the conversation. *The Vortex* had succeeded very well in London, and Arlen had been an admiring member of the opening night audience. When the play was a hit in New York as well, Coward won praise both for his writing and for his acting in the role of the neurotic, drug-addicted hero. Arlen was, of course, delighted, the more so, since the profits were so high; but a rumor started in New York that the two men were jealously feuding and barely on speaking terms. They tried to stop the rumor by dining together on every possible occasion; but, as Noel Coward recalls, "the story was then spread that our relationship was, to put it delicately, out of the ordinary. We abandoned the struggle and, like Liberace, laughed merrily on our way to our separate banks."[24]

Meantime, *The Green Hat* had opened at the Adelphi Theatre in London on September 2, 1925, with Tallulah Bankhead in the role of Iris. There too, opening night was an "event," and Miss Bankhead enjoyed great success in the role, which was for her also a breakthrough to the public. One reviewer at least was ecstatic: "Miss Bankhead is a genius," he wrote. "She does not act Iris March. She *is* Iris March." But others claimed she was inaudible for great stretches of the play; and the reviewer in the *Illustrated Sunday Herald* of September 6 said flatly, "She gave me a pain in the neck." Another detractor claimed she "neither walked, talked, looked, nor acted like a member of a County family, but more like a member of the county jail." Miss Bankhead herself dismissed the play in her autobiography as an "Armenian mishmash"—somewhat ungratefully, under the circumstances.[25]

III *Hollywood, Hard Times, and Happiness*

On October 17, 1925, Arlen left for Hollywood. He had been hired by Famous Players-Lasky Corporation, reportedly at a very high salary, to provide scenarios for film star Pola Negri, whose career was floundering after a promising beginning in Europe. A predictable publicity campaign ensued: Negri wrote of Arlen as "a genius . . . with an armor of worldly philosophy . . . to protect himself from his own sensitive nature," a man with a "secret vice of saintliness—in the matter of ideals about women."[26] In December, Arlen was quoted as saying he was gratified at her describing him as her "ideal cave man"; but he denied reports that they were to marry.[27] However, neither this publicity campaign nor her posturing at Valentino's funeral helped Negri's career, which continued to flounder; and, despite the reported high salary paid Arlen, he seems not to have produced scenarios for Negri or for anyone else.[28]

Arlen did see his short story "The Ace of Cads" turned into a successful film that starred Adolph Menjou as the natty Beau Maturin. In the 1930s and 1940s Arlen's name was associated with many films, including two adaptations of *The Green Hat*: *A Woman of Affairs* (1928) with Greta Garbo, John Gilbert, Douglas Fairbanks, Jr., and John Mack Brown; and *Outcast Lady* (1934) with Constance Bennett, Herbert Marshall, and Mrs. Patrick Campbell.

But during the years after the success of the play version of *The Green Hat*, Arlen had some difficult times. Ill health plagued him; he failed to rescue Negri's career; critics began to treat him like a man caught cheating the public; and his public turned to new interests. D. H. Lawrence wrote to S. S. Kotinsky in November, 1927, after seeing his old protégé in Italy: "Ill poor devil. . . . The Florence snobs cut him dead . . . now, after they made so much fuss of him."[29] And to Richard Aldington, Lawrence wrote of Arlen, "there's something about him I rather like—something sort of outcast, dog that people throw stones at by instinct, and who doesn't feel pious and Jesusy on the strength of it . . . but wants to bite 'em—which is good. He's one of the few people I don't mind making their pile—just to spite 'em."[30] Then working on the third version of *Lady Chatter-*

ley's Lover, Lawrence, using Arlen as his model, created the character of Michaelis, the Irish playwright who "pined to be where he didn't belong ... among the English upper classes. And how they enjoyed the various kicks they got at him! And how he hated them!"[31]

In the same year, 1927, Arlen met and fell in love with Countess Atalanta Mercati, the daughter of a Greek count and an American mother. Arlen had first seen her, he told friends, in Harry's Bar in Venice; he had asked the headwaiter for her name; and, on being told, he had said, "I shall marry her." A hectic and wracking courtship, conducted over the strong objections of her father, ended in marriage at Cannes on May 1, 1928.[32] The wedding came after the end of the social season, but many persons stayed for weeks to be present. The event was reported with unaccustomed emotions by the *New York Times*: "It was love at first sight for the novelist and his friends say that the cynical, critical Arlen of Mayfair days and continental nights changed almost overnight into a sober, serious young man with a firm belief that he was to be happier than any mortal man had ever been before."[33] Indeed, in describing his life to interviewers in later years, Arlen was fond of saying that he had, like a character in a romance, married and lived "happily ever after."

CHAPTER 6

New Directions

I Young Men in Love

T HE handicaps under which Arlen worked in resuming his career after *The Green Hat* are well illustrated by the lead paragraph of the *New York Times* review of *Young Men in Love* (1927):

> In point of actual writing, *Young Men in Love* is Michael Arlen's first novel since *The Green Hat*. Judging by the excitement of two or three years ago, when *The Green Hat* was on every drawing room table, when mention of it was on every pair of drawing room lips, and when *pour le sport* was the most familiar French phrase since *c'est la guerre*, the publication of *Young Men in Love* should prove something of an event. But though a great many people will doubtless read it, it may prove no event at all. For *The Green Hat* is now an old hat, and no longer is it fashionable or discerning to speak of Michael Arlen in the same breath with Aldous Huxley, Norman Douglas, and other writers who more permanently add to the gayety of sophisticated nations. In recent years no other author . . . has gathered round him so large an army of enthusiasts who quickly became turncoats, as Michael Arlen.[1]

From the testimony of his friends we get a sense of how nervous Arlen was about *Young Men in Love*. Beverly Nichols describes Arlen's position on his post-*Green Hat* "pedestal": "Everybody was waiting—the American publishers were waiting, the flappers were waiting, the gossips were waiting. I remember sitting, during this pregnant period, with Frederick Lonsdale, and hearing the telephone ring. Over the wire came Arlen's voice announcing that he had cut thousands of words out of his new novel. The news, in this tense atmosphere, seemed of vital importance. I wonder if it will seem of such vital importance in twenty years' time? I doubt it. And I am sure that Arlen doubts it, too."[2]

Arlen had anticipated such reactions in the pages of *Young Men in Love*. The novel's hero, Charles Savile, made a name for himself writing "clever smart, glittering books about Lords and champagne and women who went to bed with men before you could say knife" (67); but then, to the consternation of his publisher and his public, Savile turned serious and wrote "sound" novels that only the discerning enjoyed. "Savile, even at the height of his success, had known . . . that his 'success' couldn't 'last,' that he would somehow find his own level, the level where thoughtful writers wrote in decent obscurity. He knew that the day would come when the mob would dismiss him to the outer darkness as yet another of those fundamentally 'tiresome' men who cannot bring themselves to flatter the vanity of their fellows by retaining the position they have given him" (86). These lines, if we yield to the temptation of reading them as the experience of the author, are defensive, vain, and perhaps a little churlish; but they present an interesting insight into the predicament of the celebrity whose desire is to be an artist. Moreover, Savile's oft-repeated wish to be "a serious man, one of the world's workers," was, on the basis of evidence, shared by his creator and embodied in the content of the novel in which Savile appears.

The major plot of *Young Men in Love* concerns Savile's failures in his career and in love. Initially involved with a beautiful and celebrated American actress, Ysabel Fuller, who tries vainly to seduce him, Savile resists because he finds her unreal and shallow—a composite of the dramatic roles she has played and of the stances she has learned from popular literature—and because Savile, like many another Arlen character, cherishes an ideal—the ideal of a relationship that will both delight and fulfill him. Despite his resistance, Savile after a time wavers; when his career takes a downward turn, he begins to think he may be "only good enough for the Ysabel Fullers of life" (121). But at last Savile gets his chance to escape Ysabel and mediocrity through Venetia Vardon, a woman he had known when younger but had offended by his affected manners. Now thirty-seven and matured by his experiences, Savile falls in love with Venetia;

and she becomes for him "the long-awaited light in the old, old darkness" (125).

In Venetia's background and in Savile's personality there are, however, elements that finally destroy the relationship. Venetia has been intimately connected for some time with Peter Serle, a man of prominence several years older than herself—indeed, of her father's generation. Because Serle is married and a Member of Parliament, their relationship has aroused scandal that is based on the common assumption that they are lovers. In fact, however, a minimum of physical contact exists between them: Serle is sexually underdeveloped and embarrassed by the passions of both his wife and his "mistress"; and Venetia's growing interest in Savile represents a break from her stifling relationship with Serle and a chance for personal fulfillment.

Serle, trying desperately to keep Venetia, briefly resumes their sexual relationship. When the effort fails, he makes an appeal to friendship and finds unexpected allies in Savile's weakness and instability. When Venetia leaves Savile's bed one evening to visit Serle—hoping for a final discussion of their problems that will end their old relationship—Serle manages to keep her away from home well beyond the time she had promised to return. Wracked with insecurity and jealousy, Savile breaks with her after he has decided that he is not built for—cannot cope with—the kind of grand passion a relationship with Venetia would entail. At the novel's conclusion, Savile marries Ysabel Fuller and resumes writing fashionable best sellers; and Venetia marries a harmless young man who will not threaten the primacy of Serle in her life.

Through Arlen's depiction of the backgrounds to this story of failed love, he makes clear that Savile's final surrender to mediocrity is symptomatic of what was happening in society in general. Young men had come home from the war worshiping peace; they were full of "strange and unseemly visions" of a world "founded on principles of justice and pity, governed by intelligent patriots, encompassed by charity and light." At first churchmen and statesmen had encouraged their visions: "The papers were full of photographs of Mr. Lloyd George beaming with Hope at railway stations." But, with the failure of Woodrow Wilson after the Treaty of Versailles, visions of a regenerated world came to an end: "When Wilson fell, men awoke with a start to find intact the terrible inheritance of their fathers, the world we live in, the world of 'common sense' that says 'war is inevitable' because in the dawn of history one muddle-headed ass gave another muddle-headed ass a crack on the head with a stone club" (10–11).

Such a disillusioned world was made to order for men like Serle—an opportunistic politician who has made several profitable changes of party during his career—and his associates. Those associates include Venetia's financier father, Jasper Vardon, and Lord Townleigh, born Jerry Sass, who turned a fortune built on South African diamonds into a newspaper empire. In their public lives, Arlen says of the three men, "they were successful, and they made success beastly"; in their private relations, they were "the riders in the darkness around the mountain that some young people tried passionately to climb" (12).

The domestic problems of Lord Townleigh form an important subplot in the novel. "Being a Jew," Arlen writes of him, "he had brought up his children with a careful love" (39); but parenthood brings Townleigh little joy. His older son, Michael, is killed in the war; his daughter Esther bears an illegitimate child, refuses to divulge the name of the father, and lives estranged from Townleigh until her death; his younger son, Raphael, is a shaky, neurotic young man in love with Ysabel Fuller and in despair, first, about her love for Savile and, later, about her relationship with his own father, Townleigh—a situation that leads to Raphael's bungled, hysterical attempt to murder the old man. Venetia finally marries Raphael; he is the convenient and unthreatening agent through whom Venetia and Serle can continue their deadening relationship.

Much is wrong with this novel. Primarily, there is too much talk. Serle and Savile, confronted in a struggle for Venetia, for example, conduct it as a drawn-out conversation about the need for sanity in British politics. Venetia's love talk is impossible: "Those theories of yours, Charles? Oh, Charles, you've kept them all then, intact? All this time? Theories, dreams, ideals . . ." (233); "Generous Prince! Ace-Face! . . . Angel! How happy we'll be" (282). Structurally, the love affair of Savile and Venetia comes very late. The other characters—great men in the world—

are seen too much in their private roles, and little emphasis is placed upon the pressures of their public lives. A reviewer indicated this weakness when he complained of Arlen's "inability to understand that the importance of sexual facts depends on the importance of the persons involved. His lechers are ineffective in what they take to be love because they would be ineffective in anything. Fit subjects for a compassionate irony, they are treated by him as if it deeply mattered which of them slept with which."[3]

On the other hand, there is much that is well done here. In themselves, the characters are often shrewdly observed. Vardon's dying mistress, for example, is quickly but excellently portrayed as a woman who has wasted her life; old Townleigh is a full-blooded character; the rivals, Serle and Savile—the one sickly in his needs, the other befuddled by his ideals—are well characterized as men who, by the ways in which they fail Venetia, forfeit the opportunity to achieve freedom for themselves or her. All in all, Arlen was quite right to strike out in this new direction, to write of men and women who lead public lives. He had made his mark by his adroit handling of realistic material in a romantic way and of romantic materials in a cynical way. *Young Men in Love* is not a complete success, but it does try to take the full measure of its characters in their private affairs and to follow out the implications of their weaknesses and strengths.

Young Men in Love is dedicated "To Max." Friends assumed it was Beerbohm, but he claimed ignorance: "I haven't heard anything about Michael Arlen dedicating a book to me. If he does so, I shall expect a 'wide demand' for my own books to arise instantly on each side of the Atlantic. And God grant that I may keep my head!"[4] The Max referred to, however, was Max Aitken, Lord Beaverbrook, with whom Arlen had grown friendly in the years of his great success. In 1925 Beaverbrook escorted Tallulah Bankhead around London, introducing her to such friends of his as Winston Churchill and David Lloyd George. The latter, by her account, greeted her with a rose when she came to his door and had spread out on the living room floor the reviews of *The Green Hat*, in which she had recently opened.[5] That Ysabel Fuller might be patterned on Tallulah Bankhead was not suggested by contemporary reviewers, but in retrospect seems a reasonable possibility.

Reviews of *Young Men in Love* were mixed at best. The reviewer in the *London Times Literary Supplement* credited the novel with "thought as well as wit" and said it deserved sympathetic reading because of its "striving towards beauty," but he objected to its "old, curiously mingled strains of sentimentality and false cynicism."[6] Discounting the political side of the novel altogether, Mary Ross, writing in the New York *Herald Tribune*, said the novel had "all the ingredients which appeared first in 'The Green Hat,' as pleasantly cool and sparkling as freshly poured ginger ale—and reappeared in 'May Fair' and now bob up once more—each time a little less cool and sparkling, like the same ginger ale left to stand in the sun for an hour or two."[7] The *New York Times* reviewer claimed to perceive "the marks of a real deterioration on Arlen's part."[8] More negative still was the view of Thomas Beer, writing in the *Saturday Review of Literature* (New York), who accused Arlen of "posterizing" and producing, instead of characters, "figurines" which inhabit a decadent "megalopolis" in which shallow contemporary values reign.[9] Harsher yet was T. Earle Welby in the *Saturday Review* (London), who condemned Arlen's "frequent bad taste, his flashy and slovenly style, his assumption of complete knowledge of the world, his melodramatic tricks."[10]

While *Young Men in Love* is at times a grim book, it is in some ways superior to *The Green Hat* as a work of fiction. Arlen is relentless in his depiction of Savile's defeat, a defeat he makes us feel keenly but which we accept as a consequence of Savile's character. Arlen avoids all temptations to romanticize as he delineates an individual's failure of nerve, which is made to symbolize the failure of society. The difference between *Young Men in Love* and *"Piracy"*, which it somewhat resembles, is the difference between a mature, confident author who trusts his vision, and a young one who anticipates criticism by mocking his own work before his readers do. Arlen seems to have known that *Young Men in Love* could not match its predecessor, *The Green Hat*, as a best seller; but of the integrity of his own effort, he could have had no reasonable doubt.

II   The Zoo

The Zoo, a play written with Winchell Smith and published in 1927, is a comedy about marital infidelity. The title refers to various groups of partygoers, who are heard in the background of the main action, who represent "society at play." The play's heroine, Olivia Porter, is an attractive young woman with a strong moral sense who wishes not to be "modern" in her values. She has returned to the home of her stupid, party-giving mother after discovering that her husband John has had an affair. Victor Marlow, a mutual friend and her mother's guest, immediately moves to take advantage of the breakup by wooing Olivia, although he is almost dissuaded by a talk with her repentant husband. At the Act I curtain, Olivia is in Marlow's arms.

In Act II, the affair between Olivia and Victor Marlow is a week old; but John, the errant but trusting husband, suspects nothing and has naïvely asked Victor to speak to Olivia on his behalf. In the meantime, Victor has again fallen in love, this time with Olivia's young cousin, Honor. The love is returned, even though Honor is engaged to be married; and Victor passionately—and evidently sincerely—proposes marriage to both Honor and Olivia. As Act II closes, however, Olivia discovers Victor in the process of kissing Honor. In Act III, the situation is partially clarified. Olivia divines that Victor is in fact more seriously in love with Honor than with her, and she amicably returns to her husband John. Victor seems to find the actual prospect of marriage intolerable, however, and is last seen driving off at a furious speed in his automobile. Honor doesn't return to her first fiancé; at the final curtain, Olivia seems to be taking her in hand, apparently in anticipation of Victor's eventual return.

Olivia is portrayed as a thoughtful young woman determined not to succumb to the morality of her times. As she explains to her husband, her notion of marriage is "to live a quiet, decent life, not night-clubby or 'modern.'" She married John not only because he was quiet, good, and loving, but also because she was "disgusted and terrified by what is called 'society.'" She is utterly opposed to literary conventions which make the loose woman more sympathetic than the good woman: "It is a sentimental and wicked lie. . . . I shall not be laughed out of being virtuous, just because some messy modern minds have made 'being virtuous' seem ridiculous. . . . No matter what clever people say, narrow-mindedness is not so great a sin as lust" (38-39). The speech is made in Act I before her affair with Victor, but even afterwards she feels the weight of her morality; she apologizes to Victor for being a "tiresome" sinner. Her later return to domesticity is a return to her natural state, though she perhaps is chastened and made more tolerant by her own experience in adultery.

John, the husband, is a simple individual. His affair was merely a one-night stand with a woman described as a "pre-war vampire," and his remorse is quite absolute. Victor, who is more complex, is a successful portrait painter—and perhaps his passionate indecisiveness is to be ascribed to his artistic temperament. His sudden departure, which leaves the situation at the end unresolved, is consistent with his character as it has been developed.

The characterizations are pleasantly done. Comedy is provided by Olivia's mother, Mrs. Wallbridge, who seems always to have parties in progress offstage—parties attended by people she barely knows; and she protests that she can't be expected both to entertain them *and* remember their names. The play is studded with good epigrams, some old, some new, but apparently it was not effective theater: it had only a very brief run in London early in 1927 and "folded" in Pittsburgh before reaching New York later that year.[11]

III Lily Christine

The heroine of *Lily Christine* (1928) behaves outwardly in a casual, "modern" manner, apparently caring little for the standards of conduct of conventional society. Fundamentally, however, Lily Christine is a sound, good woman: as a wife and mother, she is tolerant and loving; as a friend, loyal and considerate. Both her inner virtue and her outward appearance of looseness are exploited by her husband, Ivor Summerset, a cricket idol and social celebrity. Lily Christine accepts his precarious financial state; and she dismisses his casual affairs with women she considers "pieces of nonsense." A serious

threat to their marriage occurs, however, when Summerset falls
in love with an actress, the eminently respectable Helen Abbey,
a war widow who in her public life "stood for everything that
was womanly and good and sensible" (106). Because Mrs.
Abbey, as she is called by her public, will not marry a man
against whom suit has been brought for divorce, Summerset
initiates proceedings against Lily Christine, falsely alleging
adultery on her part. Lily Christine dies, perhaps a suicide,
perhaps by accident, after finding no way to deal decently with
her situation.

Among Lily Christine's strongest supporters in her difficulties
is Rupert Harvey, an unassuming, well-meaning man who had
unwittingly provided Summerset with the basis for his charge
of adultery. Harvey had housed Lily Christine for the night
when she, a stranger, had found herself stranded near his country
home on an evening when his wife was away. A servant who
had seen Harvey in the innocent, but too casual, Lily Christine's
bedroom provides testimony later to support Summerset's false
charges of adultery. But, despite the fact that Harvey is named
corespondent in the divorce suit, he and his wife remain loyal
to Lily Christine. In describing Lily Christine to his wife,
Harvey chooses the terms *"youth, beauty, simplicity."* A lady
very much in the public eye, much photographed and admired,
liberated from superficial conventions of behavior, Lily Christine
is part of a social group whose ways puzzle the conventional
Harveys. That Lily Christine is "casual"—casual enough to stay
the night in a stranger's house, to be seen with him by servants
in a bedroom, and to greet callers to her home in her own
bedroom—disturbs Mrs. Harvey, who finds such behavior threat-
ening: "There must be a sort of punishment for casualness,
Rupert—or else everything people like me are brought up to
believe is just so much nonsense" (15). But Rupert understands
Lily Christine better; for "casualness" he substitutes "innocence."

Lily Christine had married Summerset, despite her parents'
objections, at the age of nineteen. She had loved him with
childish ardor until she was twenty-one, and then she had
settled gracefully into womanhood and motherhood. "He's not
very bright," her cousin Neville had pointed out to her. She
agreed; but her husband's lack of intelligence had made no

difference to her feelings. In later life, she tolerated the infidelities of her "old cart-horse" quite well, so long as what was between them remained unsullied. She has kept herself busy by running for a time a not very profitable dress shop and by maintaining a retinue of friends who visit her frequently. Essentially, she has accepted her husband's discreet infidelity and their genteel poverty.

Summerset has the advantages and prerogatives of class and makes use of them. His irregular income is derived mainly from gambling and from trading on his reputation as a sportsman. However, he is offended when his wife suggests that he turn professional and use his talents as a cricketer to support himself: "God, one sometimes wonders what Englishwomen are coming to!" (59). His need for his wife is profound, and he knows it; but her passion overwhelms and embarrasses him: "At the back of his mind was a dim idea that a man's wife should be on the cold side" (48). In passion, intellect, and integrity, he is his wife's inferior; finally, "He wasn't anything in particular, just a daft, selfish man who was always 'wanting' something" (294).

Mrs. Abbey is a somewhat cryptic character. Ordinary people —her public—admire her acting and respond to her public image because she gives "a convincing impression of being unspoilt and kind and good" (105). She even refuses to shingle her hair in the new fashion. The public takes pride in her as a representative Englishwoman; she is as respectable, Lily Christine acknowledges, as the Albert Memorial. At first, even the Harveys, despite their loyalty to Lily Christine, find it hard to doubt Mrs. Abbey's kindliness. But Harvey finally perceives her to be a "narrow, upright woman with a streak of righteous cruelty in her. The puritan coming out in the shop girl" (275). To Ambitriadi, a romantic but incapable admirer of Lily Christine's, Mrs. Abbey is "crafty"; to Rupert Harvey's employer, the publisher Lord Townleigh—carried over from *Young Men in Love*— she is a "devilish tricky woman." Her function in the novel is to provide a foil for Lily Christine; her deviousness and hypocrisy contrast unfavorably with Lily Christine's innocence and inner virtue.

Lily Christine's doom is brought about, ironically, by Rupert

Harvey's efforts to help her. Thinking to make her ignore her pride and force Summerset to return to her, Harvey tells her he finds the pressure of being a corespondent intolerable. But Lily Christine, determined to help her husband obtain what he wants, goes instead to another friend, the bachelor Ambitriadi, asks him to elope with her, and thus provide alternate grounds for Summerset to divorce her. When the lovelorn but frightened Ambitriadi refuses, she is defeated and is seemingly betrayed by all the males in her life. Absentmindedly walking the streets, carrying in her hands the eyeglasses she needs so badly, she is hit by a truck; and the reader is left in doubt as to whether the accident was caused by her preoccupation or was a suicide.

In *Lily Christine*, Arlen is concerned with the discrepancy between appearance and reality, especially with regard to morality. The privileged young had no standards, Harvey felt: "To them a man was not bad or good; he was amusing or a bore." This state of affairs leads Harvey to the opinion that "unless . . . we get back to some hard-and-fast standards, we shall soon be breeding a race of 'amusing' cads." The friend to whom he expresses this view responds, "*We* won't, . . . if by 'we' you mean the England that matters at all. But this particular class happens to be very busy committing suicide. I think it's a pity, as I happen to belong to it, but I don't suppose it matters in the long run if this particular kind of 'upper' class goes or not. There will always be a governing class of some kind, and it will always go rotten as it begins to be useless" (93–94). Such upper-class corruption is contrasted to the natural virtue of Lily Christine:

In their inmost consciousness they were afraid of Lily Christine, the men who loved her. And this fear was like a flower, springing from the best soil in them. They were afraid of her because her standards were instinctive, not mental or emotional or traditional. She had a criterion, instinctively. And she lived up to it, instinctively, without effort. The others, her friends, most people, were outsiders in the real sense, no matter what they were socially. . . . They were born hollow people, hollow, always waiting to be filled up with easy stuff, for easy things to be chucked into them. But you couldn't fill *her* up with the lies of tradition and prejudice and comfort, with all the little daily corruptions of life. No, you couldn't. (272)

Notable similarities exist between *Lily Christine* and *The Green Hat*: the plot device of having a glamorous woman turn up unexpectedly at night, and the sympathetic characterization of the passionate, unconventional woman subjected to unjust public condemnation, but prepared to make great sacrifices on behalf of values she superficially ignores. Moreover, many details seem, once again, to have been patterned on real people, specifically, those involved in the series of celebrated divorce suits brought by John Russell against his wife Christabel. Tabloid readers disbelieved his accusations of adultery and adopted Christabel in their hearts, through three closely followed trials, as the "typical modern girl," indiscreet but innocent.[12] However, Arlen does, as usual, make the characters his own; Lily Christine is, for the most part, a well-drawn, fully realized woman who is baffled by the follies of her husband and by the weaknesses of her friends.

Reviewers generally liked *Lily Christine*, especially those who had disliked Arlen's earlier work. "Whether it will have the success of *The Green Hat* or *Young Men in Love* remains to be seen," wrote Richard Curle in the *Saturday Review of Literature*, "but it will certainly result in Arlen's being taken more seriously. . . . If Mr. Arlen continues to develop in this manner he may well achieve a rank among the novelists that will astonish the exasperated scoffers at his earlier works."[13] The reviewer in *The New Statesman* noted "no trace of his old vulgarity and very little of false sentiment"; and he found it "exciting" that Arlen had begun "to despise the secrets of his success." He then observed that "The whole thing is written with vitality; the author is confident, the characters are true; it is a healthy, amusing, well-managed novel."[14] The *Times Literary Supplement* called the story "the best Mr. Arlen has yet told."[15] Some found fault, however, with the character of Lily Christine; the *Herald Tribune* reported her "simplified to an unnatural degree and sentimentalized";[16] and others found the ending of the book too melodramatic. Certainly, *Lily Christine* proved profitable. According to Alec Waugh, Arlen received fifty thousand dollars from *Cosmopolitan* for serial rights, and thirty-five thousand in advances from Hutchinson and Doran.[17] A movie version was

made by British Paramount in 1932 that starred Corrinne Griffith, Colin Clive, and Margaret Bannerman.

IV Babes in the Wood

Although Arlen characterizes *Babes in the Wood* (1929), a
collection of short stories, as "A relaxation intended for those
who are always travelling but never reaching a destination,"
his performance, in two of the stories at least, represents an
advance over his earlier short fiction in technique and in substance. The tone of the first story, "Confessions of a Naturalized
Englishman," is intimately autobiographical; in it, the self-
assured author, certain of his identity and his relationship to
his audience, has seemingly decided to abandon the tricks of
the romancer and tell "all" at last. Arlen speaks in the first
person; he sets his tale during World War I when as Dikran
Kouyoumdjian he was struggling with problems of recognition
and identity. At the same time, Arlen warns us in a prefatory
note that the characters in his book are fictitious: "the author
makes an appearance, but he is fictitious too"—a logical extension
of the truth, discovered by historians, that "the past is a proper
field for the imagination."

Safely hedged against accusations either of falsehood or of
abandoning romance, Arlen embarks on the story of his relationship with a girl named Priscilla, with whom he had fallen in
love a decade before. Married to a handsome but cloddish
officer of the Grenadier Guards, who had wed her for social
advancement, Priscilla nevertheless lived a Bohemian existence:
"Wanton and faithless, she was given over to regrettable pleasures with post-impressionistic poets, Bloomsbury intellectuals,
and athletic Americans" (48). Among them, she was a genuine
presence: "The influence that Priscilla had on young men is
something not to be forgotten. She was, of course, deadly to
their tranquility, binding their imaginations to her in an in-
describable commotion of love and despair and ambition. But
she was good for them, too, inspiring them with something of
her contempt for the second-rate, her humility before the spirit
of truth, and her audacious loyalties" (13).

On the first day of May, the narrator finds himself lunching with Priscilla at the Mont Agel Restaurant (a setting recalled from *"Piracy"*) discussing his career and development. She does not care for the pieces he is publishing in *The New Age* and in *The English Review*—they are not "quiet" enough—and she is beginning to think of him as the "night club type." "It's a pity...when you just conceivably might do something worth doing," she says (31). The narrator has informed us that Priscilla had nothing but contempt for ladies and gentlemen, "and so she could not be at peace but with artists and writers, or failing them, with tarts and mashers" (15); hence, she is annoyed by the narrator's search for a fashionable audience: "You are out to entertain the sort of people I detest" (32).

In defense, the narrator suggests that he lacks the background —a country, a tradition—essential to any accomplishment; and he contrasts himself with Priscilla, who has such a background in English society, even though she despises it. When she jokingly suggests that he does indeed have his own culture—nightclubs— he counters by claiming to be writing a history of Armenia. He boasts that Armenia was the location of the Garden of Eden; that Noah's Ark landed there; that it was the country of Queen Semiramis, the "inventor of eunuchs." But even this ambitious project seemingly fails to hold her interest; and when her husband—with whom she was to have been dining—comes for her, she leaves. Unexpectedly, however, she makes a secret, whispered assignation to meet the narrator for dinner.

When she fails to appear that evening at the appointed place, the narrator is utterly dejected. He goes home cursing himself and the Armenian "background" of which he had earlier boasted: "Son of an incapable race, born in the musty twilight of an outcast people, inheritor of centuries of ignoble martyrdoms and mean escapes, what did I deserve but the anxious and help-less solitude of the unwanted servant? What art could come from an Armenian? What greatness?—what, even, of worth?" (56–57). He calls Armenia an "unlovely courtesan" for having abased herself to so many conquerors. He asks, "why could you not die with dignity" like Ninevah and Babylon, thereby making a "fairly interesting corpse," instead of becoming a "bore to everyone and a burden to your children"? He characterizes Armenia's children as no more than "litter and rubbish on the face of the earth" (56–57). These lines were, taken out of context, terribly resented at the time by readers of Armenian ancestry; but, within the framework of the story, they clearly represent the narrator's temporary despair because of his personal prospects.

But, when the narrator gets home, he is amazed to find Priscilla waiting for him there. She had not been able to escape dinner with her husband's friends—"who all think I am odd and dislike me"—but she had managed to slip away after a time to see the narrator, of whose affections she was assured. Making herself at home, she stretches out on his bed and speculates about what he, as a novelist, would make of the incident they were living through. "The story to be popular would have to end up with us in each other's arms, wouldn't it? A sigh or two, teeth biting lips, and then dots . . . Oh, dear me, those dots" (73). Arlen clearly wants us to recall the similar scene in the previously published *The Green Hat*, the scene in which Iris seduces that novel's narrator: "Fingers that were not my own took the cigarette from my mouth, and teeth that were not mine bit my lip."[18]

The narrator of the short story acknowledges that the public would indeed expect such a romantic outcome—"there would be no point in the story otherwise. It would just end nowhere" (73)—but Priscilla defends sober realism: "Why not, dear? Things in life don't end in climaxes, as in stories. The stories people write are so slick, aren't they! But life isn't slick at all, things just end nowhere . . . rather beautifully, rather sadly, rather drearily, rather emptily . . . or maybe they end just as we are sitting now, talking nonsense sleepily" (73). The narrator longs to take Priscilla into his arms, but he cannot muster the courage; when at last he speaks, he finds she is asleep; and he contents himself with taking her hand: "Thus, it was written that I . . . while painfully overcoming the incredible obstacles put in a young man's way by himself, [won], on the night of the first of May, 191–, a small but encouraging triumph over the devil and a devoted friend for many years by holding, in a cramped position, Priscilla's hand while she slept for two hours and five minutes" (75–76).

Besides giving its author a chance to comment on his own

life and art, the story has value because of the welcome return of the narrator, the impoverished, ambitious, and divided young man of the early fiction. Moreover, Michael Arlen's "Confessions of a Naturalized Englishman" probably deals with his real-life relationship with Nancy Cunard, the woman he seems to have had strongly in mind when drawing Iris March of *The Green Hat* and perhaps Shelmerdene, the recurring heroine of his early short fiction. Nancy Cunard was, as we have noted earlier, the daughter of Lady Maud Cunard, who was well known in her day as a vigorous patron of the arts and as an ambitious, if somewhat eccentric, society hostess. Nancy Cunard frequently embarrassed her mother by her rebellious, freewheeling manner of life. She must have been extraordinary company, considering the number of men of talent she attracted and impressed. Her biographer, Daphne Fielding, names (besides Arlen) the poets Louis Aragon and Tristan Tzara as two men who loved her. Another young poet reportedly once threw a pistol at her feet and begged her to stop him from killing himself over her.[19]

Not all who knew her admired her, of course. Aldous Huxley drew a harsh portrait of her as Lucy Tantamount in *Point Counterpoint* (1928) and even Arlen, in "Confessions of a Naturalized Englishman," ungenerously asks, rhetorically, "Priscilla, tell me that what I hear is not true, that thy fresh loveliness is not now but a mask of ruin and paint" (7). But the range of attitudes expressed towards her merely serves to corroborate our impression of an extraordinary human presence that called forth deep and complex responses from all who knew her.

The second story in the collection, "The 'Lost Generation,'" is atypical and even distasteful, but it permits Arlen to explore characters and situations beyond his usual range. His protagonist is a businessman named Hemingway—curious choice of name!—who, while efficient, capable, and successful at his work, is "not at home in the world" (189)—not in the world of careless immorality inhabited by the young. He has an uncharacteristic affair with Beulah Ley, a woman of his own age who has, however, an "aristocratic contempt for manners" (190) which puts her in better contact with the young, as well as with artists, intellectuals, and poets. After their affair, Hemingway comes to think of her as "no more than a light woman" and leaves her.

When they meet four years later, Hemingway, hoping to re-affirm his contemptuous memory of her, instead finds his interest rekindled. At a house party he heads off a young man who, in the middle of the night, is heading for Beulah's bedroom for a rendezvous. In his jealous anger Hemingway nearly strangles Beulah, but they become, for a brief time, lovers again. Finally, however, Hemingway departs, this time for good, leaving Beulah regretful over the young lover she'd been forced to pass by.

Hemingway, appalled by Beulah's careless way of life, is not so much a moral man as an unaware man. He had "for years hidden his natural instincts beneath a mask of cool and hostile ability" and had "always been disloyal to himself in pretending to masterfulness, whereas in his heart he was a meek and lonely man" (215). Beulah, "one of the 'lost generation,' born thirty or so years ago, the children of a decaying continent . . . wan-derers without luggage" (201), does not find happiness in her "disorderly" life but could not find it in "respectability" either. Between the two characters, as between the two ways of life they represent, lies a great gulf; but in each are qualities the other lacks and misses. Despite the mutual attraction, how-ever, their differences prevail, and they cannot live together in harmony.

The remaining stories are lighter and more conventional. In "A Girl With a Future," a flighty young lady is wooed by three eligible young men; the narrator, a young Frenchman; Johnnie, an alcoholic young American; and Pepi, an enormously wealthy, handsome young Spanish Duke. After making amends for her loose existence by keeping house and doing servant's work for a blind man—a chastening but pleasurable spiritual-romantic experience—she marries the enormously wealthy Duke. "She will lead him the devil of a life. . . . He will enjoy that, and they will be very happy" (152).

In "Portrait of a Gentleman" and in "Nettles in Arcady," love blossoms inappropriately but is redirected humanely. In the former, an older man asks the young widow of a friend to marry him; she points out to him, after they have spent some time together, that he is not truly content or relaxed in her company, that he prefers the masculine atmosphere of his club. In "Nettles in Arcady," a young man falls so desperately in love with a married woman that he fails to perceive the great disparity in their ages until she makes the observation.

V Men Dislike Women

The *New York Times* review of *Lily Christine* had called Michael Arlen "an English F. Scott Fitzgerald who has still to achieve his *The Great Gatsby*."[20] The novel *Men Dislike Women* (1931) seems Arlen's effort to remedy that deficiency. Its setting and principal character are patterned quite closely on Fitzgerald's. Arlen's "Gatsby" is Charlie Macrae, an American racketeer who naïvely seeks an Ideal, a woman who will fulfill his dream of feminine purity. He seems to find such a person in an Englishwoman, Sheila Hepburn, who appears to him "a woman lonely and gracious and desperately unquiet in a world wherein a generous and tender heart was at a disadvantage" (164–65). But Sheila, "the dearest, the most unselfish, and the most stupid of women" (22), as the narrator describes her, has "led a sloppy, silly life, seeking happiness in trifling love affairs" (164). Eventually Macrae's dream is shattered. One of Sheila's former lovers tries to blackmail her, and Sheila foolishly confides about her past to a rival, Marilyn Fox, a young, spoiled American girl. When Marilyn takes advantage of Sheila's candor and tells Macrae all she has learned, the disillusioned racketeer turns from Sheila to Marilyn.

The new relationship is doomed, however, by Macrae's past. He had some years before corrupted the administration of Marilyn's father, Pete Fox, then the mayor of New York. Fox, an honest man whose career was ruined by Macrae's machinations, is determined to destroy the relationship. He plans to murder Macrae, who in his disillusionment over Sheila gives the old politician a chance to do so. But when Fox, at the moment of confrontation, finds he cannot pull the trigger, the racketeer kills himself. Sheila, though distraught, soon recovers and moves to a new romantic attachment; Marilyn marries the narrator, who has tried to reconcile the contending characters in the novel.

The narrator, a cosmopolitan individual, is Andre St. Cloud, born of a wealthy Jewish mother and a titled but impoverished French father, and educated in England. A romantic suffering from his "absorption in a life of books with a lacing of demi-monde" (21), he has come to New York to visit his brother and his brother's energetic American wife, who introduces him to her extensive social circle—thus providing Arlen with the opportunity to comment satirically on the American scene. After a few weeks of his sister-in-law's hospitality, Andre calls on the first Frenchman he meets for aid: "Do not desert me. Stay with me all afternoon. Come with me and meet Jascha Heifitz, Jack Dempsey, Artur Rubenstein [sic], Greta Garbo, Edna Ferber, John Drinkwater, George Gershwin, Andrew Mellon, Harpo Marx, Thomas Edison, and the Fratellini Brothers" (45–46).

In his efforts to escape this crowd of celebrities, Andre borrows his brother's automobile and drives across the Queensboro Bridge, which links Manhattan and Long Island. In the course of his "escape," he accidentally encounters Marilyn Fox, who takes him to Macrae's mansion in Great Neck, where a party is in progress. There celebrities also gather—drama critic Alexander Woollcott, an unnamed but unmistakable presence, is playing his favorite game, croquet—but the main object of interest for Andre is Macrae:

I saw a slight and slender man with smooth dark hair and a lean worn face. It was an attractive, leathery face. But it was not comfortable. When he was not smiling there was something sharp and harsh and reckless about him. But when he smiled he became queerly young and unsure, and he gave one the impression of being very tired from thinking the same thoughts over and over again. He had only one arm, and his movements had the faintly pathetic reckless swagger peculiar to slight one-armed men. (93)

Macrae theorizes to Andre, during their first meeting, that the institution of motherhood will save civilization, a theory which Andre finds "fatheaded," but one which does not diminish his sympathy for Macrae, especially after the racketeer has fallen in love with Sheila: "I wished him well in return for his superb innocence. He was a figure of fantasy, but what deep and opposite roots his fantasy had—in lawlessness towards men and innocence towards women" (165).

Andre, who knows of Sheila's past, never informs Macrae of it because he feels that her love is sincere and complete.

Andre tends to blame Macrae—whose feeling for women he perceives as "an outpouring of intuitive respect for a species higher than himself" (166)—rather than Sheila for their difficulties: "Galahads like you put such a high value on your respect for women that a poor mortal woman has to be a liar to win you" (277). Andre, on the other hand, sees the primacy of subjective factors in romantic relationships: "There is no such thing as 'love at first sight.' But there is in men the urge to make infinitely desirable what is immediately desirable, and so it comes to the same thing" (206–07).

Despite the many superficial similarities between *Men Dislike Women* and *The Great Gatsby*—the setting, for example; the romanticism of the central character; and the use of the Queensboro Bridge as a symbolic link between two ways of life—the differences are far more striking. Unlike Fitzgerald's profoundly obsessed character, who "invents" himself, as Nick Carraway puts it, in the confused aftermath of World War I, Macrae remains one-dimensional; he is a caricatured naïve American who is created to take part in a romance which turns into a melodrama.

As is frequently the case in Arlen's work, the truest and most interesting character is the narrator. Fitzgerald's Jewish characters stand at the disreputable periphery of his fictional world; Arlen places his in the center, thereby providing us with a cosmopolitan viewpoint from which to evaluate the characters and action. Andre's Jewishness also puts him in ironic situations. When a Jewish business associate of Macrae's tries to corner him at a party—wrongfully intruding into his cultivated second world—Macrae rudely dismisses him. Andre, looking on, reflects on the irony of the situation: "Mr. Steiner was left facing Macrae. I felt friendly towards him. Perhaps Mr. Steiner's grandfather was the same Steiner who had come over with my grandmother Schvengenstein. And now look at him. The scion of the Steiners looked desperately uncomfortable, while the scion of the Schvengensteins, in the guise of a Frenchman of means, stood leering in the offing" (193). Andre reflects further "on the childish vanity of Macrae which prompted him to talk to Mr. Steiner in the normal language of an educated man but to me in the language of the Bowery" (194); but the same kind of perverse integrity has made Andre not only flee the relative respectability of his sister-in-law's parties but also recognize a fact about himself: "I was a tramp only among orderly people, but among the unconventional I at once became orderly" (160). Andre's cosmopolitanism, of which his being Jewish is a part, becomes a universalizing attribute that connects him through his heightened sensitivities to the worlds of the innocent, the criminal, and the exotic, as well as to that of the established and conventional.

As a result, Andre is attracted to the crowds of "young newspapermen, with a sprinkling of stage people" who spend time at Macrae's apartment without inquiring too deeply into the sources of his wealth. "They were for the most part what is called an intellectual crowd. They had no God, and Ernest Hemingway was their prophet, and not such a bad prophet either. But they drank too much. This gave them a look of attractive melancholy, and women loved them. They were all going to write great novels or great plays very soon, and sometimes they did and sometimes they didn't but went to write dialogue in Hollywood. . . . They seemed to get a lot of fun out of knowing each other extremely well" (180-81).

Reviewers reacted favorably to *Men Dislike Women*. The *Times Literary Supplement* found it adroit and exciting, if anything too high in "sophisticated tension."[21] The reviewer in the *Spectator* thought it "by far his best book" and said it showed that "he is, by gifts and temperament, a serious and unusually able writer."[22] The reviewer in *Outlook and Independent* was more critical: Arlen's epigrams, "when held up for close inspection, have the substance of last year's snow," he said; but he acknowledged that the book was "readable; even the most ascetic sometimes relish a lush, green candy after meals."[23] If the book is Arlen's best, as the *Spectator* critic contended, it is only because it is less ambitious than his earlier novels. *Men Dislike Women* is a well-paced romantic melodrama with few pretensions beyond its narrator's tendency to moralize and a paragraph in the closing pages about the isolation and incompleteness of ordinary men. For the rest, the dialogue is brisk and colloquial and the characters entertaining, reflecting perhaps the influence of the light comedy of Broadway and Hollywood.

VI   Good Losers

The play *Good Losers*, written with Walter Hackett and produced at the Whitehall Theatre in London on February 16, 1931, is a comedy melodrama that opens with a Prologue set in 1917 in which three British soldiers escaping from a prison camp find their way blocked by a sentry. Randall wins the risky job of killing the sentry; and, when the other two, Doyle and Cunningham, later discover that he had cheated in order to gain the assignment, a lifelong friendship is established. Act I, which takes place years later, is set in a restaurant in which Doyle works as a cloakroom attendant and bouncer, while Cunningham is employed as a professional ballroom dancer. Randall has become a burglar and, on the evening the play opens, has been wounded during an exchange of shots with a house owner whose safe he was robbing. He has fled to Cunningham's apartment for shelter, and his two old friends try to protect him by matching wits with Chief Inspector Preston of Scotland Yard.

In Act II, Randall is discovered murdered in Cunningham's apartment; and suspicion falls on Cunningham himself when bonds from the robbery are found in his coat pocket. In Act III, a watch is kept on Cunningham's coat to see which of the guests in the restaurant will try to steal it and thus reveal himself to be the true murderer. The guilty party is revealed as Guy Hilton, the lover of the woman whose house was robbed. Hilton had seen the exchange of shots, had followed Randall to Cunningham's apartment, and had killed him in order to get the stolen bonds. Although Hilton avoids the trap set for him by Randall's friends, he is given away by the discovery of the murder weapon in his pocket. After Randall's girlfriend, Cora Drew, shoots Hilton, good-hearted Inspector Preston, a war veteran himself, helps concoct a story to explain the corpse without implicating her.

The play is quite obviously pure entertainment. The contrived plotting, conventional characterization, and "snappy" dialogue, which are competent enough for this genre, are of the sort that passed wholesale into Hollywood B movies. The main burden of comic relief is carried by Lady Frances Feather

("Frankie"), a gossip columnist who helps supply details that lead to the solution of the crime. She was played by comedienne Marion Lorne, who employed the same "fumbling" characterization she was later to use successfully for several years on American television. Ethnic humor was supplied by Anthony Holles, playing the restaurateur Balbi, who rushed about trying to pawn off superannuated pigeons on his customers. Eric Maturin, who received excellent notices for his brief portrayal of Gerald March in *The Green Hat*, was praised for his playing of Inspector Preston. Leonard Upton, who had played Napier Harpenden to Tallulah Bankhead's Iris March, was the villain Hilton.

The reviewer in the London *Times* complained of not being able at first to identify the principal characters because the stage was so crowded with restaurant patrons; he objected also that "the web of evidence is a trifle too ingeniously woven to be excitingly clear."[24] He praised Marion Lorne and the rest of the cast, however, and predicted success for the play on their account.

CHAPTER 7

Political Novelist

I Man's Mortality

"I'M through with women in love. My new novel is about politics," Arlen told an interviewer while sitting in the Miramar Bar in Cannes in 1932. "People seem to forget I'm *really* a serious writer."[1] And, indeed, despite the unlikeliness of the setting for rigorous literary activity, *Man's Mortality* (1933) is a serious work, a novel of the future in which Arlen assesses the impact of technology on civilization. The novel describes, from the vantage point of the year 2069, the events of 1987, in which a *pax aeronautica*, presided over by a powerful, autocratic combine, came to a dramatic end. The combine, International Aircraft and Airways, was founded in 1935 by ambitious transportation technologists who had gained exclusive use of anti-gravity and radar devices that guaranteed them absolute air safety and, consequently, a tremendous advantage over their competitors. Eventually Airways, as the combine came to be known, gained control of most of the world's weapons and was asked to function as its police force. As a result, although ostensibly answerable to the League of Nations, Airways in effect controlled the world with the exception of two stubborn holdouts and centers of nationalism, China and Italy. By 1987, however, management of Airways has passed to a second generation of directors—overreachers who assume more power than the world will tolerate.

In 1987 several crises occur. When Airways underhandedly seeks cause to take police action against China and Italy through the use of provocateurs, some statesmen, scientists, and Airway officers rebel against the demands of the organization. Others approach discovery of the extent to which the world's prosperity is in fact illusory, the result of manipulation of financial records

101

by the directors of Airways. But the main crisis is precipitated by the appearance of David Knox, son of the man whose inventions gave Airways its technological advantages, and a genius in his own right. In fact, David makes his father's inventions obsolete by developing highly resistant metals and a means of using air as fuel, thereby giving his aircraft unlimited range and extraordinary speed. Unlike his practical, unideological father, who had sold his inventions to the highest bidder, young Knox is a fanatic who intends to destroy the combine and its puppet the League of Nations and to unleash the dormant forces of nationalism and war. He hopes doing so will lead to the foundation of a true world government, one free of control by the managers of the transport combine.

When Knox announces his intentions, many opponents of Airways join him: Hubert Von Manteuffel, a respected Airways commander who is angered by the use of his aircraft to provoke political trouble in Italy; several talented young airmen who admire Knox's boldness and who follow Von Manteuffel; and Julian Craddock, former head of the League of Nations, at present President of England, and a believer in a true World State. A friend of the elder Knox, Craddock follows David partly to exercise a moderating influence and partly because he, too, believes that Airways' control must end before the world can create a true union of nations.

When Airways, through the League, threatens to take police action against Italy for alleged acts of nationalism and disruption, Knox, to counter this action and destroy world confidence in Airways, threatens to destroy English and French monuments—the Nelson Column and the Arch of Triumph, respectively—and publicly defies Airways to stop him. The destruction of the Nelson Column is forestalled when the courageous British cabinet, instead of evacuating the area as ordered, holds a dinner party at its base. Von Manteuffel, the humanist who values present life above the scheme of a future better state, spares them and the monument. But Knox, leading the assault himself over Paris, shows no mercy; he destroys the city and unleashes a world war. He then disappears, a probable suicide, leaving power in the hands of Von Manteuffel. This humane commander, however, is appalled at what Knox has wrought; and he realizes that the inventions left behind are too powerful to entrust to men in their present mood. He destroy's Knox's fleet, the arsenal, and the men who understand Knox's secrets. Nevertheless, the wars run their course for a decade and cause terrible devastation, but mankind eventually creates a peaceable world order.

Three characters dominate the story: Knox, Craddock, and Marie-Therese Abazar, the controlling force in Airways. She is Knox's great antagonist, and, like him, would rather see the world in ruins than abandon her goal which, unlike his, is continued Airways supremacy. Both characters are contrasted with the rumpled, unglamorous Julian Craddock who pursues his dream of a world state within a framework which values human life.

David Knox is a technological genius, like his father; but, unlike him, David is an unscrupulous visionary egotist. We understand Knox's corruptness when he tries to kill the inconveniently humane Von Manteuffel by sabotaging a plane he is to fly. Despite his respect for Von Manteuffel, whose prestige had attracted many pilots to his cause, Knox considers all men who show compassion to be of a lower species than himself.

Marie-Therese Abazar, leader of the ruling clique among the Airways Directors, mercilessly uses her position to extend her power. Her appetite for lovers is enormous, and her effect is devastating: Hemingway, her fellow director, is unable to function when she is absent; Chahine, the Armenian pilot whom she sends to spy on Knox, is passionately devoted to her, and, finally, dies in her service. Her readiness to sacrifice men to her interests ultimately leads to her downfall, however, when she deliberately sends to their death three great scientists—the only ones, Knox says, who might have duplicated his inventions—because they come close to discovering the economic frauds through which Airways has maintained the appearance of prosperity. After Knox's attack and the fall of Airways, she awaits the infuriated mob, wondering "whether the men would be enterprising enough to rape her before killing her" (267). Craddock regrets her death, however: "That unprejudiced brain of the Abazar's would have been of inestimable value in this bestial confusion. Crooks and criminals though they were, the directors had anyway been leaders, real leaders: originals, not copies; event-compelling, not event following" (271).

At several points Abazar and Knox are identified, not as lovers, because their egos would not let them meet on that level, but as equals. Craddock sees them, even when they are confronting each other in hostility, as being "of the same special order": "They were set up against each other, fighting. But in Mr. Craddock's illusion they were, in some far-away place, dissolved together into one, an indissoluble and undefeatable one" (136). Later Hemingway characterizes Abazar and Knox as "different seeming aspects of the same idea . . . not only separate from us but . . . above us." The danger represented by the Abazars and Knoxes lies in their sense of mission and the tendency in mankind to follow such leaders: "When we *are* forced to believe in a higher species, as in the case of Jesus, we make the best of a bad job by insisting that the higher species *love* us. . . . The saving vanity of man, when he is being destroyed by forces he cannot understand, tells him that his destroyer is really his saviour, and that this dying, his massacres and plagues and famines, go to build a bridge to another and higher form of life on this planet" (274). Technical superiority does not make for moral superiority, and superiority does not necessarily make one generous, as Arlen acutely indicates.

A strong theme in the book is the role of the hero-figure, the savior, in human affairs. David Knox has messianic potential; he is thirty-two years old; he attracts disciples like Von Manteuffel with an appeal that is absolute: "You and I together shall lead the fight against injustice. . . . Throw away your nets and follow me" (15). In the end, after the cross-cross bombing—the crucifixion?—of Paris, Knox walks among his followers and instructs them before his final disappearance, as though he is in a state of apotheosis. But, as the elder Knox had told Craddock in their last interview years before, being led by our betters is a risky business: "Our leaders must be representative of all our faults and weaknesses, or they will be apart from us and in the end destroy us. Didn't St. Paul do infinitely more damage than that greedy little man Napoleon? . . . Julian, the world simply cannot stand the catastrophe of another disinterested saviour" (66–67).

David regards himself as a destructive Messiah, the instrument bringing about the end of a cycle of history and permitting man to reach maturity. "I have not the patience to await crucifixion," he tells Von Manteuffel when he is preparing to leave for his mysterious death. He suggests that he is the paradox who will lead to a better life: "Men, through Judas, stumble on Jesus. Through envy, on pity. Through the destroyer, on the saviour" (251). With these words David Knox attempts to justify his historic role and the deaths of the millions in the wars he has unleashed. The final assessment of David comes from Von Manteuffel, who views him as "a mechanized Messiah": "We never took to the meek and gentle poet who called us to repentance, did we? So now we've apparently got a Messiah who speaks in a language we can understand—mathematics instead of parables, the miracle of atomic energy instead of loaves and fishes" (255). The danger lies not just in this particular Messiah; all saviors, all those who assert that they alone know the way and demand that men abandon everything to follow them, are dangerous. "There is one similarity about all Messiahs, whether they come preaching humility or electricity—they are all self-appointed. And their genius peters out in crazy self-destructive vanity—while we poor ordinary men are left to clear up the mess" (255). Slovenly and mediocre though the common man may be, he must control his own destiny.

Who then is left to fill the Messianic role? As his initials suggest, there is Julian Craddock, nondescript and all too human; he complains crankily about his feet and his rheumatism; and he retires to write in seclusion when the wars are over. He dies in 1999, after having written the history of the *pax aeronautica* and after having counted himself out of a political life that his integrity will not permit him to continue. The world which emerges from the rubble and chaos follows the humane view he sets forth: "For its first few centuries a Utopia has got to be something between a workhouse, a sanatorium, and an asylum. That's all we can hope for. That's all we deserve. And that's all we shall get. A workhouse for people tottering with childishness and an asylum for mental defectives" (280).

In writing *Man's Mortality* Arlen follows in the tradition of speculative fiction established by Jules Verne, especially Verne's

Robur, the Conqueror (also translated as *The Clipper of the Clouds*, 1886) and its sequel, *The Master of the World* (1904). In the latter book Robur, a genius who invents terrifying aerial weapons, turns misanthrope and declares war on mankind. Arlen also seems indebted to Rudyard Kipling's short story "With the Night Mail" (1905), in which is envisioned a world ruled in the year 2000 by the "Aerial Board of Control," described as a "semi-elected, semi-nominated body of a few score of persons," founded in 1949, whose motto is "Transportation is Civilisation." This board is a benign (and, in Kipling's view, necessary) dictatorship which sees its prime role as the protection of air traffic "and *all that implies*"—the final phrase containing the justification for absolute control of the world. Far from being discontented with the board, Kipling says, "our tolerant, humorous, lazy little planet [is] only too ready to shift the whole burden of public administration to its shoulders." The only hold-out, Crete, which became a tourist attraction where people might "witness the 'debates,' 'resolutions,' and 'popular movement' of the old days," succumbs gratefully in the year 2000 by demanding that the board take it under control. Kipling also produced a sequel, "As Easy as A.B.C." (1912), in which he expressed his detestation of popular government even more graphically.[2] Arlen's book goes into more psychological and physical detail than does Verne's sketchy and primitive work; and of Kipling's sardonic, mean hatred of common man, at least in the works mentioned, Arlen was, fortunately, incapable. He does, however, share the mature Verne's doubts about the absolute beneficence of technology and Kipling's view that excessive expectations based on utopian ideals may yield destructive results for society.

Arlen was also influenced by his Riviera neighbor, H. G. Wells, whose story "The Argonauts of the Air" (1897) and whose novels *When the Sleeper Wakes* (1899) and *The World Set Free* (1914), among other works, had very much earlier dealt with some of the same material Arlen used in *Man's Mortality*. But, in fact, Arlen may in some respects have "scooped" Wells, who at the time Arlen was writing *Man's Mortality* was completing one of his own visions of the future, *The Shape of Things to Come* (1933). Writing from the vantage point of 2106, Wells's historian "Philip Raven" describes a world passing through a period of insecurity (1935–1965), including a world war (1940–1950) and social disorders, followed by the organization of a group called Air and Sea Control (1965). The group, composed of pilots and technicians, gains a world monopoly on transportation. A confused but progressive era known as the Air Dictatorship follows, and by 2059 a true World State is formed, but it is one based on humane principles. In the course of delineating this vision of world history, Wells comments, through "Raven," on *Man's Mortality*, which he calls "an amusing fantasy":

It is still a very readable book and interesting in showing the limitations of the educated imagination at that time. The belief in the
possibilities of invention is unbounded; air velocities and air fighting
are described on a scale that still seems preposterously exaggerated
today; while on the other hand the inflated stock buying and selling
of that period, although it had grown from the merest germ in about
a century and a half, is represented as still going on unchanged, and
the world's air dictators are gambling dishonestly in stock, and at
last "crash" financially and bolt as though they were just contemporary politicians and mystery men rather than lords of the
whole power of the air. In a world of incredible metals, explosives
and swiftness, the Stock Exchange, the Bourses, still survive. And
there are still Powers and Foreign Policies! Nothing could illustrate
better the inability of people at that time to realize the economic
and political changes that were then actually tumbling upon them.
For some obscure reason mental and moral progress and institutional
invention seemed absolutely impossible to them.[3]

Wells shrewdly observed the unchanged economic picture Arlen represents—and certainly Arlen's device of having juggled book-keeping cause the downfall of civilization seems a weak one; on the other hand, the air velocities and the scale of warfare unfortunately seem less "preposterous" than Wells thought they would. Wells himself pulls something of a turnabout in his description of the grand passions of Jean Essenden and Elizabeth Horthy, the lovers who play for great stakes in a melodramatic interlude of the year 2106. After the downfall of Essenden, Elizabeth Horthy, in a gesture that recalls the suicide of Iris March in *The Green Hat*, throws herself from her airplane: "A mere tattered rag of body was found amidst the branches of a little thicket of oak near Chantilly" (341).

Man's Mortality received generally excellent reviews. Writing in the *Saturday Review of Literature*, Henry Tracy suggested that this novel made Arlen, long a fashionable writer, into an important one. Comparing the book to Aldous Huxley's *Brave New World* (1932), Tracy suggests that Craddock's presence adds a "saving sanity" to Arlen's book, one factor that he claimed is missing from Huxley's.[4] Most commentators noted the great distance Arlen placed between this work and his past; several noted, quite properly, the book's dedication—"to the memory of Sarkis Kouyoumdjian, merchant, of Manchester, by his youngest son"—as evidence of his serious intent. On the other hand, in a review hostile to Arlen's basic thesis, Robert Cantwell wrote in the *New Republic*, "Mr. Arlen's message is quite clear. What is the cause of the horrors evoked? The cause is the desire for peace, the desire to build a hospitable world. Disinterestedness, self-sacrifice, 'indigestible humanitarianism'—these are the impulses which, so the author believes, plunge the world into anarchy."[5]

Cantwell's point has merit; but more important is the fact that *Man's Mortality* is Arlen's most complete success in the area of serious literature. He has pursued his theme acutely and imaginatively; he has created characters who come to independent life while fulfilling their author's thematic purposes; and he has dropped his earlier stylistic affectations without sacrificing his characteristic wit.

II   Hell! Said the Duchess

Having succeeded at science fiction, Arlen next turned to allegorical fantasy with *Hell! Said the Duchess* (1934). The story concerns the lovely, chaste, and retiring widow Mary, Duchess of Dove, who rarely ventures out of her house and yet is reliably reported to be leading a life of flagrant sexual promiscuity in London. She is also implicated by circumstantial evidence in a series of "Jane-the-Ripper" murders in which male victims are sexually assaulted before being mutilated and murdered. The police and her cousin, Colonel Victor Wingless, discover that she is innocent; for she is being impersonated by a kind of succubus, a supernatural, Satanic creature named Xanthis Axaloe. Colonel

Wingless resists the sexual onslaughts of the creature and strangles it, but the experience is so devastating that Wingless commits suicide not long afterwards. The true Duchess survives.

The novel also has a political level. Arlen sets the story in the future—1938. The government had fallen, and a Conservative-Fascist coalition, led by Winston Churchill, had assumed control in 1936. Oswald Mosley became Minister of War, an event the Communists deemed provocative, and unrest had followed. As Wingless comes to perceive the affair, the Jane-the-Ripper murders are but one of series of events—including the Treaty of Versailles, the boycott of Russia, the collapse of the League of Nations, the Depression, the fall of France followed by re-establishment of a Directorate in 1936—created by some force that is attempting to cause anarchy in England. Popular anger rises when rumors circulate concerning the identity of Jane the Ripper, and the suggestion is made that, because of considerations of class, the police are shielding the Duchess from punishment. Riots and violent confrontations follow between Fascists and Communists. "This present stage of industrial development and national expansion is nearing its end," a character observes, "and mankind is drifting toward a long period of world wars" (129).

Arlen has tried to give his story metaphysical implications: when Wingless seizes the phantom by the throat, he grasps not simply the evils of murder and sexual depravity but those of war and all the troubles that have ever plagued mankind. But, despite the apparent seriousness of his intentions, Arlen fails to illuminate the evils he embodies in Axaloe; instead, he settles for melodrama and sensationalism and leaves unresolved the political issues he has raised. At the same time, Arlen reveals the Puritan element in his personality: the perverseness of the gross creature that transforms itself into a replica of Mary Dove is the only form of human sexuality portrayed in the novel. It is as if Arlen had ceased to believe that eroticism could coexist with high moral ideals, as it did in the character of Iris March, but had instead come to identify sexuality with inhuman cruelty, as he had in the character of Director Abazar in *Man's Mortality*.

Reviews were generally poor. One commentator, noting the brevity of the book, complained of "having been invited to dinner and then fobbed off with hors d'oeuvres."[6] The reviewer in the

Times Literary Supplement called Arlen unequal to the demands of his complications: "When he begins to toy with spiritual evil he is floundering beyond his depth.... He throws away his substance for a shadow—the shadow of an evil principle too paltry in its erotic aberrations to be worth evoking."[7] As has been noted above, the latter objection is justified; and the book is distinctly a minor achievement.

III   The Crooked Coronet

Arlen's last collection of short stories, *The Crooked Coronet* (1937), made up of pieces which had appeared in the popular monthly the *Strand* magazine, breaks no new ground but tries to recapture the flavor of the older, Romantic style that had brought Arlen his early success. The title story reintroduces Michael Wagstaffe, the "cavalier of the streets," who meets his match when he attempts to blackmail the charming, adulterous Lady Quorn, of whose penchant for stealing other women's men he disapproves. After several encounters, the two grow interested in each other. "You are the only man in the world who knows that I enjoy the body of love, just as a man does, and not its gentle tender spirit, as nice women are supposed to" (22), she tells him. In "The Storm Over Piccadilly" Hugo and Shirley Cypress, characters who had appeared in the earlier collections and in *The Green Hat*, have a domestic argument over a string of pearls which Hugo lends to another woman. Arlen provides a pleasant variation of de Maupassant's well-known tale "The Necklace"; his twist ending reveals that Shirley's anger is caused not by jealousy but by fear that Hugo will find the pearls are fake, the real ones having been pawned by Shirley's gambling mother.

Romantic complications provide the plot in "The Old School Tie," in which a wife makes her husband notice her by pretending to have a lover; in "The Caddish Lady's Maid," which concerns a thrice-married woman of forty-five who decides to have an affair with a young man who wishes to marry her, reasoning that through the affair she will disillusion him and thus avoid the complications of matrimony without sacrificing the pleasures of a relationship; "The Phantom of Pimlico," in which two young lovers harass the girl's father until he agrees to their marriage; and in "The Golden Ass," in which the world's richest girl for convenience marries a newspaper reporter so that she can look for a "real" husband at her leisure. The novelty of the last story derives from the fact that they do not fall in love but, on the contrary, come to dislike each other heartily.

As can be seen from the brief plot summaries given above, the stories are clearly intended as pure entertainment, and as such they succeed very well. Arlen's one venture into a deeper theme is the unfortunate story "The Black Archangel," in which George, the son of a wealthy Negro lawyer, after a visit to Africa finds work in a Hollywood movie in which he is required to fly off the Empire State Building with artificial wings. By accident he finds that, owing to some unique "Negro" muscle formation, he really can fly and returns to Africa to lead a rebellion: "I am the sword of the Lord, the black avenger. And it is I who shall uplift the black people and make them equal with the white. . . . We, the oppressed black races, shall scourge the white man and . . . punish him with fire and sword for the crimes he has committed against the sons of Ham" (126). George tells his plans to an old white drunkard named Disher, who betrays him. After his defeat, the wounded George meets Disher again; and the two fly away to commit suicide. The lesson George gains from his efforts is, as he explains to the other blacks, that "The only equality that can be between black and white is that the highest of the blacks is worthy of friendship only with the lowest of whites" (151). A more sadly inappropriate story would be hard to imagine, especially since aerial scourging in Africa in the 1930s was being provided by Mussolini's air force.

The reviews were generally favorable. The *Times Literary Supplement* and the *Manchester Guardian* especially recommended "The Black Archangel," while most others preferred the lighter stories, comparing Arlen with Saki, Evelyn Waugh, Ronald Firbank, and, most often, with P. G. Wodehouse.[8] For their wit and lightness of touch the stories generally deserve the praise they received. Readers of the *Strand* knew they could expect grace, wit, and style from Arlen, and he provided it with apparent pleasure.

IV The Flying Dutchman

In his last novel, *The Flying Dutchman* (1939), Arlen ascribes the major problems of the world—including such specific acts as the burning of the Reichstag and the revolution in Greece in 1935—to the workings of a group of anarchists and *agents provocateurs* called the Société de C., which had been formed as a piece of mischief in the 1920s and then taken over by truly evil characters in the 1930s. The organizer of the Société de C. is Chance Winter, a newspaper magnate and industrialist, who plays a "kind of criminal joke to express his contempt for so-called civilized conditions by giving men everywhere the best possible chance of misbehaving themselves" (270). When men like Armways, a cast-off participant in Lenin's revolution, and Fennerlach, a Swiss aircraft manufacturer—criminals rather than adventurers—gain control of the Société's cells in various European cities, the group turns to assassination and terrorism. Winter himself then rebels, and he secretly wipes out all the members of the organization, killing himself last of all.

The incident that changes Winter, that makes him decide to destroy his organization, is the appearance of Alfred Cherry, a weak, unstable, nervous young man who tries to sell scandalous information about his own sister, Cora Lawn, to Winter's newspapers. Cora, a famous actress, is known for the probity of her private life; and Cherry knows her career will be ruined when the public learns that their father was a notorious murderer. Curiously affected by Cherry's dreadful behavior, Winter pays for but does not print the story; and he then has a brief but public affair with Cora Lawn that causes her to break her engagement to a wealthy young nobleman. Nonetheless, the encounter with Cherry makes Winter more responsibly comprehend humanity. He and Cherry, he explains, "are the same man in slightly different form . . . versions of the same negative impulse—wasted men. Anarchistic, if you like—men full of hatred—men who *want* to attack the dignity of the human mind" (49).

Such men, Winter explains, do evil as a consequence of their own self-hate and frustrated perfectionism: "The harm in this world is seldom done by what are called 'bad men' but by men who are profoundly angry at themselves for not being as 'good'—that is to say, not as unselfishly disinterested—as they would like to be." In their frustration, these men blame the world for their own inadequacies: "The forces of disorder which are trying to tear Europe, the whole world, to pieces at this moment—their strength comes from men very much like Cherry. They want to change everything because, at bottom, they long to change themselves" (50).

Winter's way of expressing his negative impulses was, at first, to play practical jokes. In 1922, he had hired an American prostitute to pose as a great hostess and buy her way into London society; her success and his subsequent exposure of the fraud embarrassed Mayfair. The Société de C. began as a similar kind of hoax, its aim being to act as a catalyst to create disorder and discord, "to provoke the *worst* possible elements of conflicting parties by giving them excuses for violence. To provoke trouble, in short, where trouble was bound to come sooner or later" (240). When the conspirators Armways and Fennerlach gain control and for their own ends turn the organization into a terrorist group, what was an elaborate joke to Winter becomes for them a means of wrecking civilization. Finally, Winter sees, through Cherry's debasement, that he has been living his life on a false basis; he realizes the "pitiful appeal of mankind to rise above the beast and live with dignity," and this realization makes him see that he has gambled away the riches of his soul—"its humanity, its capacity for reverence" (296).

A similar process of education occurs for the narrator, Johnnie Cloud, a wastrel who had given up a career as an aircraft designer in order to marry a wealthy wife and live a life of ease. Growing restless after a while, Cloud plans a divorce and goes to work for Winter, who sees in him elements of his own character: "You gave up working, Johnnie, just to express to yourself that if the end of the world came tomorrow you would be on the reception-committee. You felt that, as a verminous civilisation was neither worth dying for nor working for, you might as well take it easy. So you decided to be a clown in a world of rats and mice" (18). But Cloud too comes to feel his human responsibilities. He aids Winter by killing Fennerlach, the most dangerous member of the Société de C, and destroying the organization's records. When Cherry betrays Winter—as Winter knew from the start he would—the founder of the Société commits suicide and thus ensures the organization's complete obliteration.

Two women play prominent roles in the action. Winter's wife, Mary, is a loyal woman, but unaware of the nature of his secret activities. She remains concerned for his welfare, even after his loss of interest in her and her growing attraction for the narrator, Cloud. Cora Lawn, her "rival," is also sympathetically drawn, though, like her brother, she is portrayed as a fundamentally flawed human being. Winter's brief affair with her, as a result of which she does not marry the man to whom she had been engaged, convinces her that she is neither a "sexual vegetarian" (171) nor intended for respectability. After Winter's departure, she becomes the mistress of a rich theatrical producer, convinced that she understands at last the true limitations of her character and ambitions.

The Flying Dutchman seems not to have been well thought out; character motivation is not always clear or consistent; the style lacks Arlen's customary bite and vigor; point of view is somewhat carelessly handled, and the narrator needs to be made aware of too many intimate conversations through unlikely channels; the Société de C. is not mentioned until the last quarter of the book, and so its importance as an explanation of evil is somewhat diluted. As a result of these flaws, reviewers found little to commend in the novel. Elmer Davis, writing in *The Saturday Review*, said it read "like a book written by a sick man who was in a hurry to get something finished before he gave out."[9] Arlen himself later confided to an interviewer that he thought it a "terrible book."[10] In any case, it was his last novel and his last book.

CHAPTER 8

Final Years

WITH the outbreak of war in 1939, Michael Arlen returned to England from the Riviera. He apparently had every intention of staying in England through the war, though his wife and, later, his children eventually were `sent for safety to North America. In November, 1939, Arlen began writing a weekly column for *The Tatler* of London. Of least interest are his efforts in the old, romantic mode; for example, "The Triumph of Spring" (March 6, 1940) begins, "Now it is quite a while since a ghost last walked through Lansdowne Passage and a nightingale last sang in Berkeley Square . . ."; but, after evoking the mood with references to his own work, he merely produces a variation on one of the stories from *These Charming People*. Much better are the pieces called "Letter to a Lady," written in the form of letters to his wife Atalanta. These are touching and often genuinely witty, as are the "Letters" of February 7 and March 27, 1940, describing visits to his son at school.

In another category altogether is Arlen's series of vigorously written patriotic and political pieces which call for greater effort in the war and for more ferocious attitudes towards the Germans. In "The Etiquette of the Thick Ear" (March 20, 1940), Arlen urges abandonment of all ideas of gentlemanly conduct or of "fair play" in the war because Germany is a ruthless, implacable enemy. In "The Man of Destiny" (February 21, 1940), Hitler is described as a pathetic man incapable of love of any sort; and in "I Lecture the Customers" (February 14, 1940), Arlen attacks Communism, and Joseph Stalin and the Dean of Canterbury are his principal targets.

One of the essays is worth quoting at length because it brings to mind the earlier, combative Arlen of the *Ararat-New Age* period. In the essay entitled "I Knew Dr. Goebbels" (January 17,

1940), he describes his spitting at Hitler's propaganda chief, George Goebbels. He had been standing, Arlen writes, on the verandah of his hotel in Athens when he saw Goebbels below, "an arrogant and intolerable little monster in whom was concentrated all the venom and corruption of this unhappy world":

It made me mad. It always makes me mad when people get away with murder and grin happily ever after. I wanted to throw a brick down at him. I wanted to spoil his nattiness for him. I wanted to knock his hat off. I wanted to forget I was a naturalized Englishman and become an Armenian again. I wanted to be a Jew and revenge all Jews.

I admire the Jews profoundly, but why have they not, regardless of all consequences, revenged themselves on monsters like Streicher and Goebbels? Why have they not done as we Armenians would have done—and did, when the Turks oppressed us? . . . The Young Turks slew us, but we slew them also. We lay in ambush and we murdered our murderers. And to teach us our lesson as slaves and dogs, they slew us in our thousands, and they raped our sisters and whipped our mothers. So we lay hidden, and murdered them one by one. . . .

To hell with suffering patiently. . . . To hell with resignation. Were I a Jew in Germany, were I a million Jews, I had rather any day be killed, as my people and their children were no longer than twenty years ago, than be made to lick a beastly German's spittle and call it honey.

And so I spat on Reichminister Dr. Goebbels' superb silk hat as he passed below me.

Arlen missed, he quickly adds—not quite anticlimactically, since the important thing was the intention, not the effect.

Early in 1940 Michael Arlen attended a dinner party at Lady Maud Cunard's home in Grosvenor Terrace. Also present, along with thirty or forty others, were Winston Churchill, soon to become prime minister, and Lord Londonderry, a prominent member of the appeasement-minded Air Ministry whose book *Ourselves and Germany* (1938) advocated friendship with Germany. Churchill was doubtless under pressure—perhaps in his cups—and angry words were exchanged when Londonderry kept pressing Churchill to read his book. Arlen unwisely interposed the opinion at this point that, from all reports, the German Air Force was quite impressive.

Churchill then turned in fury on Arlen: "You are a foreigner, an intruder, an Armenian who dares to come to this country and write books purporting to be about the manners and behavior of its aristocracy. You do not belong and never will belong to the classes in this country which you are so profitably describing. You have, in point of fact, no right to be sitting at this table." The party disintegrated; and Arlen, who described the scene to friends, was badly shaken;[1] after twenty years as Michael Arlen, a hapless chance remark, misinterpreted, had cast him again in the role of an alien.

Despite such a devastating personal attack, Arlen was determined to remain to aid the war effort. The London *Times* of November 23, 1940, announced that he had accepted an invitation by Lord Dudley to become the public relations officer for the Western Midlands.[2] Michael J. Arlen in his book *Exiles* describes his father's deep and sincere wish to serve his adopted country in its time of danger,[3] and Arlen himself wrote of his experiences and feelings in the aftermath of the devastating bombing of Coventry, which he endured. He explained how he and other government officials worked with the town council—its chairman was "a strong Socialist [who] ... had no time for nonsense"—to plan emergency measures to care for the injured and to deal with the fire and destruction. "Nothing fancy about any of them; not a leader of men in the bunch": "We were not Churchill, not Parliament, not Roosevelt, not Congress. We [were] the sovereign people. And we were governing. . . . I realized that what had happened in that room, what was happening throughout Great Britain, was the fulfillment of an age-old dream —the age-old dream that commonplace people can govern themselves without pride or jealousy or greed or cruelty. Time and time again we have been told that this is a vain dream. But I had seen it happen before my eyes."[4]

A new blow fell upon Arlen when, on January 31, 1941, a Mr. Higgs, the Member of Parliament for Birmingham, announced that the appointment of Michael Arlen to his new post was causing "considerable dissatisfaction." The Home Secretary, Mr. Morrison, was asked not only if he were aware "that Mr. Arlen was a Bulgarian" but also if he thought "the general tone of his writing made him a fit individual to hold the important

position of Public Relations Officer for the Midlands Region."
Furthermore, Mr. Higgs reminded Mr. Morrison that in his new
post Arlen "had access to confidential information."[5]

A brief article in the London *Times* of February 18, 1941,
reported that Michael Arlen had resigned his position. Not long
after this announcement, his financial holdings in England were
sequestered. "Once again," his old friend Alec Waugh recalls,
"Michael Arlen found himself, if not a man without a country,
a man without a country that would let him defend it."[6] Arlen,
who appeared to shrug off the incident, retired to his club to
relax and to play cards, Waugh recalls; but M. J. Arlen makes
clear that the experience was a painful and humiliating one for
his father.[7] Later in 1941 Michael Arlen sailed across the Atlantic
in a Brazilian freighter to rejoin his family in the United States.

Michael Arlen went to Hollywood again. With Walter Reisch,
he wrote the screenplay for *The Heavenly Body*, a comedy,
starring William Powell and Hedy Lamarr, that concerned an
astronomer who pays insufficient attention to his wife. Arlen later
downgraded his contribution, both to the movie (which wasn't
very good) and to Hollywood: "I wrote one-seventh of one
seventh-rate picture while I was there," he told an interviewer.[8]
One line in the movie is definitely his, however: when William
Powell gazes admiringly into a mirror and says, "Watch out; I'm
feeling *particularly* attractive today," he is speaking one of
Arlen's favorite lines.

"Gay Falcon," a story Arlen had written for *Ellery Queen's
Mystery Magazine*,[9] provided a character for a series of films—
fifteen in all, between 1941 and 1949, produced by Radio Keith
Orpheum, starring first George Sanders, then his brother Tom
Conway, and later some lesser lights. The hero of Arlen's story
(for whom "Gay" was a first name and not an appellative) was
a desperate character who is rather like a more mature, sardonic
Michael Wagstaffe. Hollywood turned him into a romantic
rogue; the series had a profitable run; and although Arlen wrote
no scripts for it, he received credit as "author." Arlen also worked
on—or told people he was working on—a play to be entitled "The
Humble Peacock," which was to be a portrayal of the American husband.

Michael Arlen moved from Hollywood to New York in 1945.

Alec Waugh describes the last years of Arlen's life as a comfortable round of long lunches with old friends at the St. Regis, the Colony, and other locations in New York. Through the memoirs of his son, Michael J. Arlen, we see that these years had another aspect, for they were clouded by Arlen's frustration and disappointment. Like many of the restless young men of his novels, he liked to be involved and active, to make his voice heard; and he who had caused headlines by merely arriving in a city could not have been fond of obscurity. Hopefully he found solace and reward in knowing he had achieved enormous popular success and conducted his public career with grace; while the testimony of friends demonstrates the affectionate regard they had for him as a person. He died of lung cancer in New York on June 23, 1956.

II *Conclusion*

Michael Arlen began his writing career as a spokesman for an uprooted, scattered people who were living through a national catastrophe. By temperament, however, he was not suited for such a role and his ambition and talents led him into other directions. Personal inclination and the advice of his mentors brought him, after a period of exploration and self-examination, to the role of Romancer. The transition occurred on the pages of A. R. Orage's *The New Age*, and the final portion of the transition is seen in the "London Papers." The candor and charm with which Arlen faced himself in these articles gives *The London Venture* permanent vitality. But his commercial success in the early 1920s was the result of his talent for writing clever Romantic fiction, sprinkled with epigram, in a knowing, sophisticated tone. He could and occasionally did pursue serious themes, as in "The Romance of Iris Poole" and *The Green Hat*, but he usually chose not to probe the issues these works raised. There is some justice to the comment of W. C. Frierson, who wrote in the early 1940s of Arlen's Romances that "the most an indulgent critic may today affirm is that Arlen's writings were sometimes graceful even when they were ornate; that they possessed a certain technical efficiency, borrowed from Maupassant and the elliptical method of Conrad, which put the reader on his mettle; and that they are of historical importance in showing the partiality of a war-conscious generation for a manner of mild decadence, a precise and exotic discrimination, a flavor of sin."[10] A more sympathetic commentator might, while finding merit in Frierson's analysis, point out that the stories are often extremely successful entertainment; that their wit is real and considerable; that in them Arlen creates a distinctive world of sparkling characters who remain a pleasure to visit; that the stories are told through a distinctive, genial narrative personality, the creation of which is in itself a remarkable achievement.

And yet, a part of Arlen, it is clear, yearned to be "one of the world's workers" and a "serious" author. When he turned to broader concerns in his later novels, he did so through an exploration of the nature of evil. In *Young Men in Love*, the sterility of Peter Serle, who controls and stifles Venetia, also afflicts English politics; while the well-meaning but futile Charles Savile ends by losing integrity both in art and love. *Man's Mortality* suggests that mankind has much to fear from those who come arrogantly to its salvation and that men of ordinary capacity and temperament are its best hope. *Hell! Said the Duchess* points to Satanic origins for human woes, but the novel simplistically identifies evil with sexuality. *The Flying Dutchman* probes the notion that the greatest harm is done by men who hate themselves and therefore cannot comprehend the potential for dignity in their fellow men. Of them all, *Man's Mortality* is his best work because Arlen has his narrative skills in order, drops affectations, and explores his themes through an exciting, bold plot. Arlen did not, with these books, repeat the extraordinary commercial success of his earlier efforts, but he was honestly coping with problems to which he had in the past given only conventional answers.

Still, of all the stories Michael Arlen told, the best was his own. The most significant conflict of his life—the one with the most universality—was related to his efforts to be part of a society that, despite his understanding of its limitations and flaws, attracted him all his life and that never fully accepted him, despite all the ways he found to serve it. In his writing, he never really confronted directly his conflict with himself and with society, but the attractive, vigorous outlaws in his stories—the "Cavalier of the Streets," Michael Wagstaffe; the "Ace of Cads," Beau Maturin; the "Prince of the Jews," Julian Raphael; and the others, perhaps even Iris March herself—manifest Arlen's perceptions about alienation. These characters, in their gameness, their desperate nobility, their firmly held private codes which serve as alternatives to the values of society, gain power by reflecting the conflict within Arlen.

Finally, to assess Arlen's achievement and account for his popularity we must return to the narrative voice in his stories and, through that voice, to Arlen himself. His contribution was not to the analysis of society, to the discussion of the "Woman Question," or to the development of narrative form, though he gave conscious thought to these subjects. Rather, his achievement lies in the special rapport he established with his audience through a narrative voice which was the vehicle for wit and genial satire. We may regret that in his creative life he was a man of passion who settled for being a man of style; but he remained, in his books as in life, supremely good company.

Notes and References

Chapter One

1. [Geoffrey Hellman], "Loller," *New Yorker*, XXV (April 9, 1949), 25.

2. My principal sources for Arlen's early life are his *The London Venture* (London, 1920); the short story "Confessions of a Naturalized Englishman" in *Babes in the Wood* (London, 1929); and Michael J. Arlen, *Exiles* (New York, 1970). Other sources are: Alec Waugh, *My Brother Evelyn and Other Portraits* (New York, 1967); Daphne Fielding, *Those Remarkable Cunards* (New York, 1968); Paul Selver, *Orage and the New Age Circle* (London, 1959); Alexander Frere, "The Myth of Mayfair Society," *Books and Bookmen* (London), II (August, 1956), 24.

3. Selver, p. 62.

4. *The London Venture*, pp. 128–30.

5. Ibid., pp. 130–32.

6. Ibid., pp. 16–18.

7. Ibid., p. 18.

8. Fielding, p. 54.

9. Harry T. Moore, ed., *The Collected Letters of D. H. Lawrence* (New York, 1962), I, 396.

10. Witter Bynner, *Journey With Genius* (New York, 1951), p. 199.

11. *The Collected Letters of D. H. Lawrence*, I, 414.

12. "Confessions of a Naturalized Englishman," p. 5.

13. Hugh Ford, ed., *Nancy Cunard: Brave Poet, Indomitable Rebel* (Philadelphia, 1968), p. ix. She may have known, and made a pun from, the Armenian word *bah-ron*, which means, simply, "mister," but which has been mistaken for a grander title.

14. Alexander Frere, "The Myth of Mayfair Society," p. 24.

15. For a good summary of the circumstances, see Marjorie Housepian, "The Unremembered Genocide," *Commentary*, XL (September, 1966), 55–61.

16. "An Appeal to Sense," *Ararat: A Searchlight on Armenia* (London), IV (July, 1916), 22.

17. "The Young Armenian," ibid., IV (August, 1916), 89.

18. "The Very Serious Armenian," ibid., IV (September, 1916), 142.

19. *The London Venture*, pp. 84–85.

20. Selver, p. 63.

21. Marmaduke Pickthall, "The Literature of Turkey" (Letter), *New Age*, XXV (May 1, 1919), 15.

22. "The Function of Daggers," *New Age*, XX (January 11, 1917), 259.

23. Gorham Munson, *The Written Word*, rev. ed. (New York, 1962), p. 70. Munson, whose source was Arlen himself, recounts that Orage set Arlen the task of writing out his recollections at top speed in order to develop fluency. When Arlen reached one hundred and fifty thousand words, "he threw the manuscript aside" (p. 102) and went on to write the series that became *The London Venture*.

24. "Michael Arlen: A Fragment of a Novel," *New Age* (August 9, 1917), 332. Richard Aldington suggests that the true subject of the "Fragment" is D. H. Lawrence and that Arlen wrote it in annoyance. See *Portrait of a Genius, But . . .* (London, 1950), p. 178.

25. Alec Waugh, *My Brother Evelyn*, p. 260.

26. *The London Venture*, p. vii.

Chapter Two

1. Haik was the legendary founder of Armenia; hence, *Hayastan*, the Armenian name for Armenia.

2. Alec Waugh, *My Brother Evelyn*, p. 256.

3. "An Armenian in London," *New York Times Book Review* (July 18, 1920), p. 27.

4. Andrew Turnbull, ed., *The Letters of F. Scott Fitzgerald* (New York, 1963), p. 182.

5. Ernest Hemingway, *A Moveable Feast* (New York, 1964), p. 175.

6. *The Green Hat* (London, 1924), p. 69.

7. Richard Aldington, *Life for Life's Sake* (New York, 1941), p. 147. Aldington also recalls that Arlen once offered to repay a publisher for that portion of his advance which his book had not earned —a notable departure from general practice.

8. Herbert Van Thal, ed., *The London Venture*, introduction by Noel Coward (London, 1968), p. x.

9. Grant Overton, *Cargoes for Crusoes* (New York, 1924), p. 272. See also, David Martin, "Arlenesque," *Bookman*, LX (November, 1924), 293–94.

10. See Vincent Sheean, *Dorothy and Red* (Boston, 1963), p. 38.

Also mentioned in the same passage is a "Lady [L.]," with whom Arlen is supposed to have had a youthful affair.

11. See Tallulah Bankhead, *Tallulah* (New York, 1952), pp. 134–39.

12. Daphne Fielding, *Those Remarkable Cunards* (New York, 1968), p. 74.

13. See John Lodowick, *Gulbenkian: An Interpretation of "The Richest Man in the World"* (Garden City, N.Y., 1958); and Nubar Gulbenkian, *Pantaraxia* (London, 1965).

14. George Doran, *Chronicles of Barabbas: 1884–1934; Further Chronicles and Comment: 1952* (New York, 1952), p. 178.

15. " 'Piracy,' " *Spectator*, CXXX (January 20 1923), p. 108. This review mentions the existence of advertisements for a sequel to *"Piracy,"* suggesting that Arlen had considered continuing the story of Ivor and Pamela.

16. "Latest Works of Fiction," *New York Times Book Review* (May 27, 1923), p. 11.

17. Gerould Gould, "New Fiction," *Saturday Review*, CXXXIV (November 18, 1922), 761.

18. Mr. Cerf very kindly supplied these details in a letter to the author, dated December 2, 1969.

Chapter Three

1. *These Charming People* (London, 1923), p. iii.

2. *May Fair* (London, 1925), p. iii.

3. "New Novels," *Times Literary Supplement* (June 28, 1923), p. 438.

4. Herman J. Mankiewicz, "And Thus and Thus Writes Mr. Arlen," *New York Times Book Review* (May 31, 1925), p. 5.

5. Francis Melville Perry, *Short Story Writing: Lessons from the Masters* (New York, 1926), p. 221.

6. E. L. Pearson, "The Mysteries of Success," *Outlook*, CXL (June 10, 1925), 221.

7. The intensity of Arlen's vogue is demonstrated by the following account, very graciously provided by Daphne Fielding in a letter to the author dated July 4, 1970: "I was under the spell of his books in my late-teens, and I once popped a Cartier cigarette case to give a clandestine dinner-party in a small Soho restaurant, where all the girls wore green hats—(bravely worn they were) and we talked and behaved like characters in *These Charming People*."

8. *May Fair*, p. 11. In *The London Venture* Arlen wrote, "I am only half-heartedly a realist, and may yet live to be accused of shuffling humanity behind a phrase" (139).

9. Doran, *Chronicles of Barabbas*, p. 179.

10. *The Romantic Lady* (London, 1921), p. 4.

11. Ibid., p. 111.

12. Alec Waugh, *My Brother Evelyn*, p. 260.

13. Herman J. Mankiewicz, "Mr. Arlen Speaks Respectfully of Mr. Arlen," *New York Times Book Review* (March 22, 1925), p. 2.

14. *Babes in the Wood*, pp. 37–38.

15. Edwin Bjorkman, "These Charming People," *Literary Digest International Book Review*, II (December, 1923–November, 1924), 476. The same elements are emphasized by Hans Carl Guggenbuhl in *Michael Arlen: Kritiker der englischen Gessellschaft* (Zurich, 1937), pp. 13–21 and 35–59.

16. *May Fair*, pp. 36–58.

17. Ibid., pp. 166–201.

18. Ibid., pp. 116–32.

19. *These Charming People*, pp. 51–62.

20. Ibid., pp. 283–302.

21. *May Fair*, pp. 251–275.

22. *These Charming People*, pp. 91–103.

23. Ibid., pp. 165–77.

24. *The Romantic Lady*, pp. 85–107.

25. *These Charming People*, pp. 178–201.

26. *May Fair*, pp. 59–94.

27. *These Charming People*, pp. 63–90.

28. Ibid., pp. 120–44.

29. Ibid., pp. 202–25.

30. Ibid., pp. 104–19.

31. *May Fair*, pp. 224–50.

32. Ibid., pp. 276–326.

33. Ibid., pp. 202–23.

34. Ibid., pp. 95–115.

35. *The Romantic Lady*, pp. 35–81.

36. *These Charming People*, pp. 226–37.

37. *The Romantic Lady*, pp. 111–41.

38. *These Charming People*, pp. 247–82.

39. See, for example, Edwin Bjorkman, "These Charming People," op. cit. See also "Some Lovely Ladies," *New York Times Book Review* (March 30, 1924), p. 9.

40. *My Best Story: An Anthology of Stories Chosen by Their Own Authors* (Indianapolis, 1930).

41. *May Fair*, pp. 133–65.

42. Ibid., pp. 327–69.

43. Beverly Nichols, *The Sweet and Twenties* (New York, 1958).

In *Those Remarkable Cunards,* another of Lady Cunard's introductions is recorded: "This is Mr. Evan Morgan, who looks like the poet Shelley and whose mother makes birds' nests" (52). Ivor Marlay is described to Magdalene Gray in nearly these words in *"Piracy",* p. 86.

44. *May Fair,* p. 345.

45. Consuelo Vanderbilt Balsan, *The Glitter and the Gold* (New York, 1952), p. 200.

Chapter Four

1. Claude Carlos Washburn, *Opinions* (London, 1926), p. 63.

2. Daphne Fielding, *Those Remarkable Cunards,* p. 74. There were other candidates as well. Writing in the late 1920's, Rebecca West suggested the name of Mona Tattersall: "It was largely the life she and her friends had led round and about the Embassy Club in London, the Potinière at Deauville, and the Sporting Club at Monte Carlo, which made Michael Arlen write *The Green Hat* and other people read it." See *Ending in Earnest: A Literary Log* (Freeport, New York, 1967), p. 17. When asked by an interviewer about the model for Iris March, Arlen responded, "She never lived ... so far as I know.... She's just made up of ever so many, many different people I've really met and known." (Herman J. Mankiewicz, "Mr. Arlen Speaks Respectfully of Mr. Arlen," p. 2.)

3. *Nancy Cunard: Brave Poet, Indomitable Rebel,* p. ix.

4. "Civilized Emotion," *New York Times Book Review* (September 21, 1924), p. 9.

5. Stark Young, "The Green Hat," *New Republic,* XLIV (September 30, 1925), 153.

6. Clarence Bray Hammond, "An Audacious Author," *Saturday Review of Literature,* I (October 4, 1924), 159.

7. "The Green Hat," *Times Literary Supplement* (June 19, 1924), p. 386.

8. Elizabeth A. Drew, *The Modern Novel: Some Aspects of Contemporary Fiction* (New York, 1926), p. 62.

9. George Jean Nathan, "Mr. Arlen," *American Mercury,* VI (November, 1925), 373–74.

10. W. Y. Tindall, *Forces in Modern British Literature: 1885–1956* (New York, 1956), p. 103.

11. Barry Pain, *This Charming Green Hat-Fair* (New York, 1926), p. 64.

12. Eric Frisch, *Arabella* (London, 1933), title page.

13. Corey Ford, "Three Rousing Cheers!!! The Parody Adventures

of Our Youthful Heroes, The Rollo Boys with Sherlock in Mayfair or, Keep It Under Your Green Hat," *Bookman*, LXIII (January, 1926), 584.

14. *Life Magazine*, LXXXIV (January 1, 1925), 11.

15. Pola Negri, "My Neighbor, Mr. Arlen," *New York Times* (December 20, 1925), Sec. VII, p. 6.

16. Relevant to this subject are observations in Q. D. Leavis, *Fiction and the Reading Public* (London, 1932), concerning best-selling authors "trying to interpret the workings of a personality stated but not shown to be cultivated and complex" (242); the tendency of such authors "to depend on stock responses which enable them by a few clumsy strokes to evoke a composite picture that is already stowed away in their readers' minds" (243); the use of "attitudes formed round the words 'noble' and 'pure' and the idea of self sacrifice for its own sake" which writers borrowed from popular Victorian poets and "incorporated into popular ideology" (245); the "excursion[s] into profundity" which the writer takes us on before "we come back to the comfortable axioms of *l'homme moyen sensuel*" (251).

17. Svetlana Alliluyeva, *Twenty Letters to a Friend*, trans. Priscilla Johnson, McMillan (New York, 1967), p. 113.

Chapter Five

1. "Dear Father," *Times* (London), December 1, 1924, p. 10.

2. "Mr. Arlen's Charming People," *New York Times* (October 7, 1925), p. 31.

3. Principal sources for this chapter are: Katherine Cornell, *I Wanted to be an Actress* (New York, 1938); George Doran, *Chronicles of Barabbas*; and, of inestimable value, the Scrapbook of the American run of *The Green Hat*, held in the Theater Collection of the New York Public Library (cited here as Scrapbook).

4. Cornell, pp. 75–77; cf. Guthrie McClintick, *Me and Kit* (Boston, 1955), p. 239.

5. Doran, p. 180.

6. Burton Rascoe, "Contemporary Reminiscences," *Arts and Decorations*, XXIII (May, 1925), 45.

7. "Arlen Addresses Armenian Educational Foundation," *New York Times* (March 25, 1925), p. 25.

8. "Mayfairian," *Time*, IX (May 2, 1927), 39.

9. Doran, p. 183.

10. Ibid., p. 180.

11. Alec Waugh, *My Brother Evelyn*, p. 262.

12. See Cleveland Amory and Frederic Bradlee, eds., *Vanity Fair: Selections from America's Most Memorable Magazine* (New York, 1960), p. 102.

13. Cornell, p. 78.

14. Michael Arlen, *The Play Version of the Green Hat* (New York, 1925). An abbreviated version appears in Burns Mantle, ed., *The Best Plays of 1925–26* (New York, 1926), pp. 121–59.

15. Cornell, p. 79. A discrepancy exists between printed text and this recollection, but Miss Cornell was obviously the authoritative witness as to what was actually said on stage.

16. Ibid.

17. Ibid., p. 80.

18. Alexander Woollcott, "Plays and Players in These Parts: 'The Green Hat' as Chicago and Detroit Know It." The review, labeled "*New York Sun*, April, 1925," is preserved in the Scrapbook.

19. An advertisement preserved in the Scrapbook reads: "The dramatic sensation of the century. The triumph of fiction becomes the triumph of fashion, and the Green Hat—symbol of sophisticated chic —is now available to the woman of smart individuality."

20. Louis Bromfield, "The New Yorker," *Bookman*, LXI (November, 1925), pp. 320–21.

21. All reviews quoted appear in Cornell, pp. 221–27, or in the Scrapbook.

22. Leslie Ruth Howard, *A Quite Remarkable Father* (New York, 1959), pp. 106–7.

23. Cornell, p. 82.

24. H. Van Thal, ed., *The London Venture*, p. x.

25. Bankhead, *Tallulah*, p. 174.

26. Pola Negri, "My Neighbor, Mr. Arlen," *New York Times* (December 20, 1925), Sec. VII, p. 6.

27. "Arlen Denies He'll Wed," *New York Times* (December 29, 1925), p. 19.

28. In *Memoirs of a Star* (Garden City, New York, 1970), Pola Negri mentions a film called *The Crossroads of the World*, "an original story by Michael Arlen" (262). The same film was announced in *Theater* magazine, XLIII (January, 1926), 31. However, the film seems not to have been made.

29. *The Collected Letters of D. H. Lawrence*, II, 1024.

30. Ibid., p. 1023.

31. D. H. Lawrence, *Lady Chatterley's Lover* (New York, 1959), p. 22.

32. Cf. the account in Michael J. Arlen, *Exiles* (New York, 1969), pp. 25–26.

33. "Michael Arlen Weds Countess in Consulate," *New York Times* (May 2, 1928), p. 17; see also, "Church is Thronged for Arlen Wedding," *New York Times* (May 3, 1928), p. 19.

Chapter Six

1. Louis Kronenberger, "Mr. Arlen's Green Hat Grows Dusty," *New York Times Book Review* (May 1, 1927), p. 9.
2. Beverly Nichols, *Are They the Same at Home?* (London, 1927), p. 31.
3. T. Earle Welby, "New Fiction," *The Saturday Review*, CXLIII (April 30, 1927), 676.
4. Rupert Hart-Davis, ed., *Max Beerbohm's Letters to Reggie Turner*, with an Introduction by the editor (New York, 1965), p. 264.
5. *Tallulah*, p. 168.
6. "Young Men in Love," *Times Literary Supplement* (May 19, 1927), p. 352.
7. Mary Ross, "Mr. Arlen on the Vulgarization of Failure," *Books* (*New York Herald Tribune*) (May 1, 1927), p. 2.
8. Kronenberger, "Mr. Arlen's Green Hat Grows Dusty," p. 9.
9. Thomas Beer, "Notes on Megalopolis," *Saturday Review of Literature*, III (May 14, 1927), 819.
10. Welby, "New Fiction," p. 676.
11. "Rialto Gossip," *New York Times* (October 16, 1927), Sec. IX, p. 1.
12. See the account in John Collier and Iain Lang, *Just the Other Day: An Informal History of Great Britain Since the War* (New York, 1932), pp. 175–77.
13. Richard Curle, "A New Vision of a Woman," *Saturday Review of Literature*, V (November 17, 1928), 369.
14. "New Novels," *New Statesman*, XXXII (February 2, 1929), 533.
15. "New Novels," *Times Literary Supplement* (February 14, 1929), p. 116.
16. Mary Ross, "Michael Arlen's 'Good Woman,'" *Books* (*New York Herald Tribune*) (November 18, 1928), p. 3.
17. Alec Waugh, *My Brother Evelyn*, p. 263.
18. *The Green Hat*, p. 54.
19. For this entire account, I am indebted to Daphne Fielding, *Those Remarkable Cunards* (New York, 1968), pp. 57–68, 93–95. Ms. Anne Chisholm, who is writing a biography of Nancy Cunard, informs me, in a letter dated September 14, 1974, that she has found, in the extensive collection of Nancy Cunard's papers at the University of

Texas, a "long account of her friendship with Arlen and what he was like then and what her other friends thought of him. . . . It is very vivid and quite revealing." To my great regret, I have not had the opportunity to consult this document.

20. "Mr. Arlen's Syrup," *New York Times Book Review* (November 18, 1928), p. 6.

21. "Men Dislike Women," *Times Literary Supplement* (April 2, 1931), p. 272.

22. L. A. G. Strong, "Mr. Arlen and Others," *Spectator*, CXLVI (April 4, 1931), 553.

23. [Virgilia Peterson Ross], "The New Books," *Outlook and Independent*, CLVII (April 15, 1931), 536.

24. *Times* (London) (February 16, 1931), p. 9.

Chapter Seven

1. Derek Patmore, "Conversations in the South," *Bookman*, LXXXII (August, 1932), 370.

2. "With the Night Mail" appears in the collection *Actions and Reactions* (London, 1905); "As Easy as A.B.C." appears in *A Diversity of Creatures* (London, 1912).

3. H. G. Wells, *The Shape of Things to Come* (New York, 1933), p. 339.

4. Henry Tracy, "The New Michael Arlen," *Saturday Review of Literature*, IX (April 8, 1933), 525.

5. Robert Cantwell, "Man's Mortality," *New Republic*, LCCIV (April 12, 1933), 252. Other significant reviews include: "War in the Air," *New York Times Book Review* (March 26, 1933), pp. 15–16; Mary Ross, "Michael Arlen's World of 1987," *Books* (*New York Herald Tribune*) (March 26, 1933), p. 6.

6. Iris Barry, "New Fiction," *Books* (*New York Herald Tribune*) (November 4, 1934), p. 20.

7. [Anonymous], "Fiction," *Times Literary Supplement* (July 5, 1934), p. 477.

8. [Anonymous], "The Golden Ass," *Times Literary Supplement* (August 14, 1937), p. 591; Harold Brighouse, "The Crooked Coronet," *Manchester Guardian* (August 17, 1937), p. 5; P. M. Jack, "The Crooked Coronet," *New York Times* (November 21, 1937), p. 24; Rose Feld, "The Crooked Coronet," *Books* (*New York Herald Tribune*) (November 21, 1937), p. 14.

9. Elmer Davis, "Reading Matter," *The Saturday Review*, XX (July 22, 1939), 10.

10. John Keating, "Michael Arlen, Esq." *Cue*, XIX (July 1, 1950), 12.

Chapter Eight

1. Vincent Sheean, to whom Arlen recounted the incident, provided the details in a letter to the author dated October 28, 1970.

2. *Times* (London) (November 23, 1940), p. 2.

3. Michael J. Arlen, *Exiles*, p. 37.

4. Michael Arlen, "The People Write on Stone," *Saturday Evening Post*, CCXIV (December 27, 1941), 25.

5. *Times* (London) (January 31, 1941), p. 9.

6. Waugh, *My Brother Evelyn*, p. 266.

7. Michael J. Arlen, *Exiles*, p. 37.

8. John Keating, "Michael Arlen, Esq." p. 12.

9. Reprinted in *To the Queen's Taste* (Boston, 1946), pp. 344–66.

10. William Coleman Frierson, *The English Novel in Transition: 1885–1940* (Norman, Oklahoma, 1952), p. 267.

Selected Bibliography

PRIMARY SOURCES

1. *Works signed Dikran Kouyoumdjian*

A. The following appeared in *Ararat: A Searchlight on Armenia,* published by the Armenian United Association of London:

"An Appeal to Sense," IV (July, 1916), 18–22.
"The Young Armenian," IV (August, 1916), 89–91.
"The Very Serious Armenian," IV (September, 1916), 141–42.
"War and Art," IV (October, 1916), 187–89.
"Sic Semper Tyrannis," IV (December, 1916), 277–78.
"Kings and Queens," IV (February, 1917), 374–77.

B. The following appeared in the *New Age* (London), edited by Alfred R. Orage:

"An Appeal to Sense," XIX (August 3, 1916), 322–23.
"The Decline of Humour," XIX (September 7, 1916), 448–49.
"New Lamps for Old," XIX (October 19, 1916), 595.
"Clever Mr. Cannan!" XX (November 9, 1916), 38.
"Sic Semper Tyrannis," XX (December 7, 1916), 136–37.
"The Function of Daggers," XX (January 11, 1917), 258–59.
"A Note on Bacon," XX (February 1, 1917), 328–29.
"Figures in a Room," XX (April 5, 1917), 539.
"A Defence of Tailors," XXI (May 3, 1917), 16–17.
"Tigranes the Slave," XXI (June 14, 1917), 161–63.
"On the Art of Being Oppressed," XXI (June 28, 1917), 207–208.
"Michael Arlen: A Fragment of a Novel," XXI (August 9, 1917), 330–32.
"The Courtesan of the East," XXII (February 28, 1918), 349–51.
"London Papers I. Ave," XXIII (August 15, 1918), 253–55.
"London Papers II. Salve," XXIII (September 5, 1918), 303–5.
"London Papers III. Vale," XXIII (October 3, 1918), 367–69.
"London Papers IV," XXIV (November 7, 1918), 7–9.
"London Papers V," XXIV (December 5, 1918), 76–77.

"London Papers VI," XXIV (December 19,1918), 108–9.
"London Papers VII," XXIV (January 9, 1919), 162–64.
"London Papers VI [sic]," XXIV (February 20, 1919), 261–63.
"London Papers," XXV (May 15, 1919), 43–46.
"London Papers," XXV (May 22, 1919), 64–68.
"Mr. Pickthall and Armenia," [Letter], XXV (May 22, 1919), 70–71.

2. *Works signed Michael Arlen*

A. Novels (listed in order of publication)

The London Venture. Drawings by Michel Sevier. London: William
   Heinemann, Ltd., 1920; New York: George H. Doran Co., 1920.
   An edition dated 1919, issued by Heinemann, is extant, but it
   was in fact issued after the edition of 1920. See *Publishers
   Weekly,* December 5, 1924, p. 1823.
"Piracy": A Romantic Chronicle of These Days. London: W. Collins
   Sons & Co., Ltd., 1922; New York: George H. Doran Co., 1923.
The Green Hat: A Romance for a Few People. London: W. Collins
   Sons & Co., Ltd., 1924; New York: George H. Doran, Co., 1924.
Young Men in Love. London: Hutchinson & Co., Ltd., 1927; New
   York: George H. Doran Co., 1927.
Lily Christine: A Romance. London: Hutchinson & Co., Ltd., 1928;
   New York: George H. Doran Co., 1928.
Men Dislike Women: A Romance. London: William Heinemann,
   Ltd., 1931; Garden City, N.Y.: Doubleday, Doran & Co., 1931.
Man's Mortality: A Story. London: William Heinemann, Ltd., 1933;
   Garden City, N.Y.: Doubleday, Doran & Co., 1933.
Hell! Said the Duchess: A Bed-Time Story. London: William Heine-
   mann, Ltd., 1934; Garden City, N.Y.: Doubleday, Doran & Co.,
   1934.
The Flying Dutchman: A Novel. London: William Heinemann, 1939;
   Garden City, N.Y.: Doubleday, Doran & Co., 1939.

B. Short Stories, Collected (listed in order of publication)

The Romantic Lady. London: W. Collins Sons & Co., Ltd., 1921;
   New York: Dodd, Mead and Co., 1921. Contains "The Romantic
   Lady," "Fay Richmond," "Consuelo," and "The Romance of Iris
   Poole."
These Charming People. London: W. Collins Sons & Co., Ltd., 1923;
   New York: George H. Doran Co., 1924. Contains "Introducing
   a Lady of No Importance and a Gentleman of Even Less,"
   "When the Nightingale Sang in Berkeley Square," "The Hunter

After Wild Beasts," "The Man with the Broken Nose," "The Luck of Captain Fortune," "The Ancient Sin," "The Cavalier of the Streets," "Major Cypress Goes Off the Deep End," "Consuelo Brown," "The Irreproachable Conduct of a Gentleman Who Once Refused a Knighthood," "Salute the Cavalier," "The Shameless Behavior of a Lord," "The Loquacious Lady of Lansdowne Passage," "The Smell in the Library," and "The Real Reason Why Shelmerdene Was Late for Dinner."

May Fair. London: W. Collins Sons & Co., Ltd., 1925; New York: George H. Doran Co., 1925. Contains "Prologue," "A Romance in Old Brandy," "The Ace of Cads," "Where the Pigeons Go to Die," "The Battle of Berkeley Square," "The Prince of the Jews," 'The Three-Cornered Moon," "The Revolting Doom of a Gentleman Who Would Not Dance with His Wife," "The Gentleman from America," "To Lamoir," "The Ghoul of Golders Green," and "Farewell, These Charming People."

Babes in the Wood: A Relaxation for Those Who Are Always Travelling But Never Reaching a Destination. London: Hutchinson & Co., Ltd., 1929; Garden City, N.Y.: Doubleday, Doran & Co., 1929. Contains "Confessions of a Naturalized Englishman," "A Girl With a Future," "Portrait of a Gentleman," "The 'Lost Generation,' " and "Nettles in Arcady."

The Crooked Coronet and Other Misrepresentations of the Real Facts of Life. London: William Heinemann, Ltd., 1937; Garden City, N.Y.: Doubleday, Doran & Co., 1937. Contains "The Legend of the Crooked Coronet," ". . . of the Golden Ass," ". . . of the Bearded Golfer," ". . . of the Storm over Piccadilly," ". . . of the Black Archangel," ". . . of the Caddish Lady's Maid," ". . . of the Policeman in Pince-nez," ". . . of the Old School Tie," ". . . of the Phantom of Pimlico," ". . . of the Agreeable Widower," ". . . of the Gorilla of Mayfair."

C. Short Stories, Uncollected (listed in order of publication)

"The Dead Half-Hour," *English Review*, XXX (January, 1920), 19–28. (Reprinted, with a satirical ending, as "When The Nightingale Sang in Berkeley Square" in *These Charming People*.)

"The Fall of Lady Toni," *English Review*, XXX (April, 1920), 336–47.

"Tea at the Ritz," *Smart Set*, LXVI (December, 1921), 127–28. (A variation, told from a different narrative point of view, of "The Luck of Captain Fortune" from *These Charming People*.)

"Lark Among Crows," *Everybody's Magazine*, L (January, 1924), 175–79.

"Punctilious Parbald," *Everybody's Magazine*, L (March, 1924), 25–30.

"The Sheik of Alabam," *Everybody's Magazine*, L (April, 1924), 41–48.

"Salute Mr. Lancelot," *Redbook*, XLIV (December, 1924), 42–45, 136–38.

"One Gold Coin," *Bookman*, LX (January, 1925), 556–64; and LX (February, 1925), 699–709.

"The Legend of Isolda," *Redbook*, XLIV (March, 1925), 38–41, 107–110.

"The Hand and the Flower," *Redbook*, XLV (May, 1925), 46–49, 122–24.

"The Knife Thrower," *Redbook*, XLV (July, 1925), 46–49, 135–40. (A variation of "The Prince of the Jews" from *May Fair*, in which the title character is Armenian rather than Jewish.)

"Portrait of a Lady With Grey Eyes on Fifth Avenue," *Liberty*, II (January 16, 1926), 7–8.

"Portrait of a Girl on Hollywood Boulevard," *Liberty*, II (February 20, 1926), 22–24.

"Why Men Join Clubs," *Redbook*, XLVII (August, 1926), 68–71, 146.

"Eyes of the Blind," *Redbook*, XLVII (September, 1926), 54–57, 106.

"Love in Eternity," *Redbook*, L (January, 1928), 39–41, 130–35.

"The Great Emerald Mystery," *Redbook*, L (February, 1928), 49–51, 90–94.

"First Love," *Liberty*, VI (April 20, 1929), 13–22.

"O Chivalry!" *Liberty*, VI (July 20, 1929), 13–22. (An early version of the novel *Hell! Said the Duchess*.)

"An Affair of the Heart," *Cosmopolitan*, LXXXVI (October, 1929), 76–79, 117–25.

"Transatlantic," *Liberty*, VIII (May 16, 1931), 7–11.

"A Young Man Comes to London." London: J. J. Keliher and Co., Ltd., 1931. (Brochure for the opening of the Dorchester Hotel, London.)

"Gay Falcon," *To the Queen's Taste . . . the best Short Stories Published in . . . Ellery Queen's Mystery Magazine*. Edited by Ellery Queen. Boston: Little, Brown & Co., 1946. Pp. 344–66.

D. Magazine Articles

The following appeared in *The Tatler* (London):

"An Appeal to Women," LIV (November 8, 1939), 198.

"On Worms," LIV (November 15, 1939), 220.

"Letter to a Lady," LIV (November 22, 1939), 254.

"How to Avoid Being Divorced," LIV (November 29, 1939), 286.

"Lament for the Last War," LIV (December 6, 1939), 332.

"The Love Life of Bimbo Carruthers," LIV (December 13, 1939), 360.

"The Chastity of Murderers," LIV (December 20, 1939), 398, vi.

"Confessions of a Self-Made Man: Startling New Year Revelations," LV (January 3, 1940), p. 16.

"Letter to a Lady," LV (January 10, 1940), 48.

"I Knew Dr. Goebbels," LV (January 17, 1940), 80.

"Portrait of a Pretty Girl," LV (January 24, 1940), 116.

"Rouge Over England," LV (January 31, 1940), 146.

"Letter to a Lady," LV (February 7, 1940), 184.

"I Lecture the Customers," LV (February 14, 1940), 218.

"The Man of Destiny," LV (February 21, 1940), 248.

"Gorillas Know Best," LV (February 28, 1940), 282.

"Triumph of Spring," LV (March 6, 1940), 316–17.

"The Best People Dine at 8:45," LV (March 13, 1940), 350.

"The Etiquette of the Thick Ear," LV (March 20, 1940), 384.

"Letter to a Lady," LV (March 27, 1940), 418.

"All Men Salute the Senior Service," LVI (April 3, 1940), 18.

"A Marriage Has Been Arranged," LVI (April 10, 1940), 54.

"An Injured Husband," LVI (April 24, 1940), 144.

"Last Week's Big Divorce," LVI (May 1, 1940), 184.

The following appeared in the *Saturday Evening Post*:

"The People Write on Stone," CCXIV (December 27, 1941), 25.

E. Plays (unpublished)

"Dear Father." Starred Herbert Marshall, Isabel Jeans. Produced at The New Scala Theatre, London, November 30, 1924. (Reviewed in the *Times* (London), December 1, 1924, p. 10.)

"These Charming People." Starred Cyril Maude. Produced at the Gaiety Theater, New York, October 6, 1925. A revision of "Dear Father." (Reviewed in the *New York Times*, October 7, 1925, p. 31.)

"Why She Was Late for Dinner." Produced at the Everyman Theatre, London, November 27, 1926. A dramatization of the story "The Real Reason Why Shelmerdene Was Late for Dinner" from the book *These Charming People*. (Reviewed in the *Times* (London), November 27, 1926, p. 9.)

F. Plays (published)

The Acting Version of The Green Hat, A Romance. New York: George H. Doran Co., 1925. Portions reprinted in *The Best Plays of 1925–26.* Edited by Burns Mantle. New York: Dodd, Mead & Company, 1926.

The Zoo: A Comedy in Three Acts. Written in collaboration with Winchell Smith. New York: Samuel French, Inc., 1927.

Good Losers: A Play in Three Acts and a Prologue. Written in collaboration with Walter Hackett. New York: Samuel French, Inc., 1933.

G. Screenplays

The Heavenly Body. Written in collaboration with Walter Reisch. 1944. Metro-Goldwyn-Mayer. Stars: William Powell, Hedy Lamarr, James Craig, Fay Bainter. Director: Alexander Powell. (Reviewed in the *New York Times,* March 24, 1944, p. 17.)

H. Films based on his novels or stories

Dancer of Paris. 1926. First National. No star. Directed by Alfred Santell. (Reviewed in the *New York Times,* January 31, 1926, Sec. VII, p. 5; and March 29, 1926, p. 24.)

The Ace of Cads. 1926. Famous Players-Laski. Star: Adolph Menjou. Director: Luther Reed. Adaptation and screenplay: Forrest Halsey. (Reviewed in the *New York Times,* October 24, 1926, Sec. VIII, p. 7.)

A Woman of Affairs. 1928. Metro-Goldwyn-Mayer. Stars: Greta Garbo, John Gilbert, Douglas Fairbanks, Jr., John Mack Brown. Director: Clarence Brown. Scenarist: Bess Meredyth. Based on *The Green Hat.* (Reviewed in the *New York Times,* January 21, 1929, p. 18; and on January 27, 1929, Sec. IX, p. 7.)

These Charming People. 1931. Stars: Cyril Maude, Godfrey Tearle, Nora Swinburne, Ann Todd. Director: Louis Mercanton. Screenplay: Hugh Perceval, Irving Howard. Film version of the play "Dear Father" (as produced in London) or "These Charming People" (as produced in New York).

Lily Christine. 1932. Stars: Corinne Griffith, Colin Clive, Margaret Bannerman, Miles Mander. Director: Paul Stein. (Reviewed in the *New York Times,* May 29, 1932, Sec. VIII, p. 4.)

Outcast Lady. 1934. Metro-Goldwyn-Mayer. Stars: Constance Bennett, Herbert Marshall, Mrs. Patrick Campbell, Hugh Williams. Director: Robert Z. Leonard. Screenplay: Zoe Akins. Based on

The Green Hat. (Reviewed in the *New York Times*, November 3, 1934, p. 20.)

The Golden Arrow. 1936. First National. Stars: Bette Davis, George Brent, Eugene Pallette, Dick Foran. Director: Alfred E. Green. Screenplay: Charles Kenyon. (Reviewed in the *New York Times*, May 4, 1936, p. 16.)

The Falcon Series: *Gay Falcon,* 1941; *Date with the Falcon,* 1941; *The Falcon's Brother,* 1942; *The Falcon Takes Over,* 1942; *The Falcon Strikes Back,* 1943; *The Falcon and the Co-Eds,* 1943; *The Falcon in Danger,* 1943; *The Falcon in Hollywood,* 1944; *The Falcon in Mexico,* 1944; *The Falcon Out West,* 1944; *The Falcon's Alibi,* 1946; *The Falcon's Adventure,* 1947; *Devil's Cargo,* 1948. Radio-Keith Orpheum. Stars: George Sanders, Tom Conway. Also *Search for Danger,* 1949, for Falcon Productions.

I.   Translations of Arlen's works

Armenian: *Gananch Klkharge* [*The Green Hat*]. Translated by Hermine P. Isgender. [Publisher unlisted], 1926.

Dutch: *De Groene Hoed* [*The Green Hat*]. Amsterdam: P. N. Van Kampen, n.d.

French: *Le Feutre Vert* [*The Green Hat*]. Translated by Lucette Caron Culbert. Paris: Librairie Plon, 1928.

German: *Als die Nachtigall sang.* Translated by E. I. Schiffer. Munich: R. Piper, ca. 1935. Selected stories from *These Charming People.*

   De Grüne Hut [The Green Hat]. Translated by Willy Seidel. Berlin: Ullstein, n.d.

   Lily Christine: Roman. Translated by Else Baronin Werkmann. Leipzig: C. Weller & Co., 1930.

Hungarian: *A Sold Kalap, regency* [*The Green Hat*]. Translated by G. Beke Margit [No other information available.]

Italian: *Gente Piacevole* [*These Charming People*]. Translated by E. Grossi-Bellezanti. Milan: Modernissima, 1930.

Lettish: *Lilija Kristine* [*Lily Christine*]. Translated by Velta Spara. Riga: "Gramatu draugs," 1937.

Polish: *Zielony Kapeluez: powiesc dla wybranych* [*The Green Hat*]. [No other information available.]

Swedish: *Den Grona Hatten: en roman för de utvalda* [*The Green Hat*]. Translated by Siri-Thorngren-Olin. Stockholm: H. Gelber, 1925.

J.   Reprints of collections and novels

Ghost Stories. London: W. Collins Sons & Co., Ltd., 1927.

The Man with the Broken Nose and Other Stories [from *These*

Charming People]. London: W. Collins Sons & Co., Ltd., 1927.
The Ace of Cads and Other Stories [from *May Fair*]. London: W. Collins Sons & Co., Ltd., 1927.
Young Men in Love. London: Universal Library Co., 1929.
The Ancient Sin and Other Stories [from *These Charming People, May Fair*, and *The Romantic Lady*]. London: W. Collins Sons & Co., Ltd., 1930. Reissued, 1931.
"Piracy". London: W. Collins Sons & Co., Ltd., 1932.
The Romantic Lady and Other Stories. London: The London Book Co., 1933.
These Charming People. London: Penguin Books, 1937.
The Green Hat. Introduction by A. S. Frere. London: Cassell & Co., Ltd., 1968.
The London Venture. Edited by Herbert Van Thal. Introduction by Noel Coward. London: Cassell & Co., Ltd., 1968.

K.   Reprints of individual short stories in anthologies

"The Ancient Sin" in:

More Ghosts and Marvels. Edited by Vere Henry Collins. London: Oxford University Press, 1929.
Strange and Fantastic Stories. Edited by J. A. Margolies. New York: Whittlesey House, 1946.

"The Battle of Berkeley Square" in:

The Evening Standard Book of Strange Stories. London: Hutchinson & Co., Ltd., 1934.

"The Cavalier of the Streets" in:

Bedside Book of Famous British Stories. Edited by Bennett Cerf and H. C. Moriarty. New York: Random House, 1940.

"Dancer of Paris" in:

World's Best Short Stories of 1925. New York: George H. Doran Co., 1926.

"Gay Falcon" in:

To the Queen's Taste. Edited by Ellery Queen. Boston: Little, Brown & Co., 1946.

"The Gentleman from America" in:

Ghostly Tales to be Told. Edited by Basil Davenport. New York: Dodd Mead and Co., 1950.
Great Ghost Stories of the World. Edited by A. K. Laing. Toronto: Blue Ribbon, 1941.
Great Short Stories of Detection, Mystery, and Horror. 1st series. Edited by D. L. Sayers. London: V. Gollancz, 1929.
The Haunted Omnibus. Edited by A. K. Laing. New York: Farrar and Rinehart, 1937.
Great Tales of Terror and the Supernatural. Edited by H. A. Wise and P. M. Fraser. New York: Random House, 1944.
Omnibus of Crime. Edited by D. L. Sayers. New York: Payson and Clarke, 1929.

"The Ghoul of Golders Green" in:

The Mammoth Book of Thrillers, Ghosts, and Mysteries. Edited by P. M. Parrish and John R. Crossland. London: Odham's, 1938.

"The Legend of the Crooked Coronet" in:

Introduction to Modern English and American Literature. Edited by W. S. Maugham. Philadelphia: Blakiston, 1943.

"The Luck of Captain Fortune" in:

The Evening Standard Book of Best Short Stories. 2nd Series. London: Search Publications, 1934.

"The Man with the Broken Nose" in:

Fifty Modern English Writers. Edited by W. S. Maugham. Garden City, N.Y.: Doubleday, Doran & Co., 1933.
The Traveller's Library. Edited by W. S. Maugham. Garden City, N.Y.: Doubleday, Doran & Co., 1933.

"The Prince of the Jews" in:

My Best Story. Indianapolis: Bobbs-Merrill, 1930.

"The Shameless Behavior of a Lord" in:

Georgian Stories. London: Chapman and Hall, 1925.

"The Smell in the Library" in:

The Great Book of Thrillers. Edited by H. Douglas Thomson. London: Odham's, 1937.

The Best British Short Stories of 1923. Edited by E. J. O'Brien and J. Cournos. Boston: Houghton Mifflin, 1924.

"Was He a Liar?" in:

The Evening Standard Book of Best Short Stories. London: Search Publications, 1933.

SECONDARY SOURCES

Critical studies, reminiscences, background works, parodies, and significant reviews.

ABINGDON, ROGER. *The Green Mat: A Romance of Askew People.* London: W. Collins Sons & Co., Ltd., 1925. Parody.

AGATE, JAMES. *The Contemporary Theatre: 1925.* London: Chapman & Hall, Ltd., 1926. Contains a chapter on the London production of *The Green Hat.*

ALDINGTON, RICHARD. *Life for Life's Sake: A Book of Reminiscences.* New York: The Viking Press, 1941. Arlen recalled with affection and respect.

ARLEN, MICHAEL JOHN. *Exiles.* New York: Farrar, Straus and Giroux, 1970. Powerful, deeply personal memoir of Arlen's later years written by his son.

BANKHEAD, TALLULAH. *Tallulah.* New York: Harper & Brothers, 1952. Little on Arlen, but much that is of interest on mutual acquaintances, such as Lords Alington and Beaverbrook.

CORNELL, KATHERINE. *I Wanted to be an Actress.* New York: Random House, 1938. Invaluable recollections of the stage success of *The Green Hat.*

COWARD, NOEL. *Present Indicative.* Garden City, N.Y.: Doubleday, Doran and Co., 1937. Arlen recalled with affection.

DEMPSEY, DAVID. "I Didn't Quite Catch . . . ." *New York Times Book Review,* February 15, 1953, p. 8. Interview.

DONALDSON, FRANCES. *Freddy Lonsdale.* London: William Heinemann, 1957. Contains a number of anecdotes about Arlen.

DORAN, GEORGE H. *Chronicles of Barabbas, 1884–1934; Further Chronicles and Comment, 1952.* New York: Rinehart & Co., 1952. Informative but not wholly accurate view of Arlen by his American publisher. Arlen is hailed as a Jewish Realist.

DREW, ELIZABETH. *The Modern Novel: Some Aspects of Contemporary Fiction.* New York: Harcourt, Brace and Co., 1926. Finds Arlen's style wanting, but ascribes the success of *The Green Hat* to its plea for a single sexual standard.

FIELDING, DAPHNE. *Those Remarkable Cunards: Emerald and Nancy.* New York: Atheneum, 1968. Valuable description of Arlen's early milieu and the personality of Nancy Cunard, the model for Iris March.

FORD, COREY. "Three Rousing Cheers!!! The Parody Adventures of Our Youthful Heroes. The Rollo Boys with Sherlock in Mayfair or, Keep It Under Your Green Hat." *Bookman*, LXIII (January, 1926), 583–88. Parody.

FORD, HUGH, ed. *Nancy Cunard: Brave Poet, Indomitable Rebel.* Philadelphia: Chilton Books, 1968. Nancy Cunard recalled and described by friends. Two pages from *The Green Hat* are included, along with several incidental references.

FRERE, ALEXANDER. "The Myth of Mayfair Society." *Books and Bookmen*, II (August, 1956), 24. Affectionate obituary by a friend from the earliest days in London; makes the necessary point that Arlen was not a Realist, but that he influenced the behavior of his readers.

GOULD, BRUCE. "Farewell to These Charming People." *Literary Digest International Book Review*, III (December, 1924–November, 1925), 399–400. Extended review of *May Fair*.

GUGGENBUHL, HANS CARL. *Michael Arlen: Kritiker der englischen Gesellschaft.* Zurich: Affoltern am Albis, 1937. Concentrates on Arlen's ideas on society, marriage, family, and other topics.

[HELLMAN, GEOFFREY.]"Loller." *New Yorker*, XXV (April 9, 1949), 24–25. Interview with Arlen comfortably retired in New York.

HOWARD, LESLIE. "Such is Fame." *New Yorker*, I (November 14, 1925), 16–17. Humorous glimpse backstage at the Broadway production of *The Green Hat*.

––––––. "Intimate Diary of an Opening Night." *New Yorker*, I (October 31, 1925), 13–14. Humorous account of the opening night of *The Green Hat* by a member of the cast.

HOWARD, LESLIE RUTH. *A Quite Remarkable Father.* New York: Harcourt, Brace and Co., 1959. Contains an amusing description of Leslie Howard's problems playing Napier in the New York production of *The Green Hat*.

KEATING, JOHN. "Michael Arlen, Esq." *Cue*, XIX (July 1, 1950), 12. Interview concerning a projected television series for which Arlen was to be host. Only one performance was televised.

LESLIE, SHANE. "Michael Arlen Makes London Shudder." *Literary Digest International Book Review*, II (December, 1923–November, 1924), 769–70. Extended review of *The Green Hat*.

LOVETT, ROBERT MORSS. "Some Lines on Mr. Arlen." *New Republic*, (December 10, 1924), 8–9. Review of Arlen's career up to *The Green Hat*.

McCLINTICK, GUTHRIE. *Me and Kit*. Boston: Little, Brown, and Co., 1955. Katherine Cornell's husband and director describes her success in *The Green Hat*.

MANKIEWICZ, HERMAN J. "And Thus and Thus Writes Mr. Arlen." *New York Times Book Review*, May 31, 1925, p. 5. Extended review of *May Fair*.

————. "Mr. Arlen Speaks Respectfully of Mr. Arlen." *New York Times Book Review*, March 22, 1925, p. 2. Informative interview in which Arlen discusses his technique as a writer.

MARTIN, DAVID. "Arlenesque." *Bookman*, LX (November, 1924), 293–94. Review of Arlen's career; cites gossip concerning *"Piracy"*.

MARTIN, WALLACE. *The New Age Under Orage*. New York: Barnes and Noble, 1967. Consideration of one of Arlen's early benefactors and advisors.

"Michael Arlen." *Theatre*, XLI (May, 1925), 10, 60. Informal interview with Arlen in London during rehearsals of *The Green Hat*.

"Michael Arlen: He Is the Harold Bell Wright of Sophisticates." *Time* (September 22, 1924), 13. Compares Arlen condescendingly to the prolific American author of moralistic best sellers.

MORLEY, SHERIDAN. *A Talent to Amuse: A Biography of Noel Coward*. Garden City, N.Y.: Doubleday & Co., Inc. 1969. Describes the early friendship of Arlen and Coward; also Arlen's role in financing the *Vortex*.

NATHAN, GEORGE JEAN. "The Theatre: Mr. Arlen." *American Mercury*, VI (November, 1925), 373–74. Review of *The Green Hat*, with caustic general comments on Arlen's style and content.

NICHOLS, BEVERLEY. *Are They the Same at Home?* London: Jonathan Cape, 1927. Describes Arlen's decline in reputation.

NOOSE, MELITA. [pseud.] *Young Women Out of Love: Being a Commentary on the Genius Peculiar to Michael Arlen*. London: Stanley Paul & Co., 1928. Parody.

OVERTON, GRANT. *Cargoes for Crusoe*. New York: Appleton & Co.; George H. Doran Co.; Boston: Little, Brown and Co., 1924. Promotional volume, with chapters on authors represented by these publishers, including one on Arlen.

PAIN, BARRY. *This Charming Green Hat-Fair*. New York: Adelphi Co., 1926. Parody.

"Past Masters." *Time*. XLVII (February 11, 1946), 44. Interview with Arlen in New York.

PATMORE, DEREK. "Conversations in the South." *Bookman*, LXXXII (August, 1932), 370–71. Interview in Cannes; concerns serious intentions of *Man's Mortality*.

PEARSON, EDMUND LESTER. "The Mysteries of Success." *The Outlook*, CXL (June 10, 1925), 221. Extended review of *May Fair*.

PERRY, FRANCIS MELVILLE. *Story-Writing: Lessons from the Masters*. New York: Henry Holt and Co., 1926. Contains a chapter on Arlen's short-story technique.

RIDDELL, JOHN. "Men Dislike Arlen." *In the Worst Possible Taste*. New York: Charles Scribner's Sons, 1932. Parody.

SAROYAN, WILLIAM. "The Armenian Who Almost Didn't Want to Be an Armenian." *Ararat* (New York), XI (Autumn, 1970), 2–5. Perceptive and revealing commentary on Arlen as an influence and as a friend.

SELVER, PAUL. *Orage and the New Age*. London: George Allen & Unwin, Ltd., 1959. Amusing view of Arlen in his early days.

SHAND, JOHN. "An Explorer in Mayfair." *Living Age*, XLII (April 10, 1926), 109–112. Critical view of Arlen's alleged lack of Realism and moral values.

SITWELL, OSBERT. *Three-quarter Length Portrait of Michael Arlen*. London: William Heinemann, Ltd., 1930. Poem-portrait; commissioned by Arlen.

WASHBURN, CLAUDE CARLOS. "Sophistication." *Opinions*. London: Constable & Co., Ltd., 1926. Attack on Arlen and Ford Madox Ford; critical of style, subject matter, and falsity of stories to real life.

WAUGH, ALEC. *My Brother Evelyn and Other Portraits*. New York: Farrar, Straus, and Giroux, 1967. Contains an affectionate memoir of Arlen; charming and informed.

Index

147